Royal Shakespeare Company

The Royal Shakespeare Company is built around a core of Associate Artists (actors, directors, designers) who, by working together over long periods with shared ideas, aim to achieve a distinctive style. It was formed twenty-two years ago and under the leadership of Peter Hall at Stratford-upon-Avon and later that same year, 1960, it took over the Aldwych Theatre as its London headquarters. Audiences in the capital were then able to see Shakespeare productions from Stratford alongside both new plays and classics at the Aldwych.

In 1974 the Company's range of work expanded yet again with the opening of The Other Place in Stratford, a small auditorium where Shakespeare and contemporary writers could be staged in more intimate surroundings than had been hitherto possible at either the Royal Shakespeare Theatre or the Aldwych. Its London counterpart, The Warehouse, opened in 1977, with a policy of staging the best new plays by modern British writers, such as — in recent seasons — Howard Barker, Edward Bond, Howard Brenton, David Edgar, Barrie Keeffe, Tom McGrath, David Mercer, Mary O'Malley, Stephen Poliakoff and Peter Whelan. From time to time this work receives a wider audience on transfer to a larger theatre such as the Aldwych or to the West End, as recently in the case of Pam Gems' *Piaf* (from The Other Place), Willy Russell's *Educating Rita* and C P Taylor's *Good* (both from The Warehouse).

In the RSC's new London home in the Barbican Centre for Arts and Conferences, the direct descendant of The Warehouse is The Pit, an auditorium with flexible seating for up to 240 people.

Despite box office figures for all its theatres, which have no equal anywhere in the world, the RSC cannot recoup its expenditure from ticket sales alone. It relies on assistance each year from the Arts Council of Great Britain, who remain the Company's only source of public subsidy. This subsidy amounts to about one-third of the Company's costs for a year's work — the shortfall must be recovered by work in other media and, ever-increasingly, by commercial sponsorship.

The Body

by
Nick Darke

RSC Playtext   Methuen/RSC

First published as a paperback original in 1983 by Methuen London Ltd.,
11 New Fetter Lane, London EC4P 4EE in association with the
Royal Shakespeare Company

Copyright © 1983 by Nick Darke

The original music for the Royal Shakespeare Company's production of *The Body* was composed by Guy Woolfenden. Parts and scores, and details concerning performing rights in the music are available from Guy Woolfenden, c/o The Royal Shakespeare Theatre, Waterside, Stratford-upon-Avon, Warwickshire CV37 6BB.

ISBN 0 413 53340 9

CAUTION
This play is fully protected by copyright. All rights are reserved and all enquiries concerning the rights for professional or amateur stage productions should be made to Margaret Ramsay Ltd., 14a Goodwin's Court, St Martin's Lane, London WC2N 4LL. No performance may be given unless a licence has been obtained.

This paperback edition is sold subject to the condition that it shall not, by way of trade or otherwise, be lent, resold, hired out, or otherwise circulated without the publisher's prior consent in any form of binding or cover other than that in which it is published and without a similar condition including this condition being imposed on the subsequent purchaser.

Characters

THREE FARMERS OF THE PARISH
MRS MAY
STANLY, *her husband*
ARCHIE GROSS
KENNETH, *his son*
GRACE, *Kenneth's wife*
GILBERT, *Grace's brother*
ALICE, *Gilbert's fiancée*
RECTOR
MAVIS RICKEARD
BENNY
GRACE'S MOTHER
MANNY COCKLE
THE BIG FOUR COMBO
A BODY
LIEUTENANT
WALT
AL

Prologue

Three FARMERS *of the parish address the audience.*

FARMERS:
We, the farmers of this parish,
Do admit
The presence of
American units
On our airbase.
We look out across
Our meadows
And count
Nuclear weapons
Amongst our sheep.
We speak with one voice
And keep our collective
Mouth on the subject shut.
We have no choice,
We know that.
And we gaze with mild disapproval
Upon those who seek their removal.

One of our number, Kenneth, sat with his wife one morning, before breakfast.

KENNETH *removes himself from the* FARMERS' *group and sits with his wife,* GRACE. *She joints a bullock.*

KENNETH: Grace, I fancy mushrooms for breakfast.

GRACE: Then pick some.

KENNETH: I think I might. That's what I was thinking.

GRACE: Did you milk the cows?

KENNETH: Yes.

GRACE: Feed the pigs?

KENNETH: Yes.

GRACE: Count the sheep?

KENNETH: Yes.

GRACE: Collect the eggs?

KENNETH: Yes.

GRACE: Grease the combine?

KENNETH: I can't grease the combine Grace, not before breakfast, on an empty stomach.

GRACE: Then don't leave it for me to do at the last minute. I can't reach the nipples. There's nipples on that combine was put in places a cockroach couldn' reach.

KENNETH: My arms is too thick. Yours is thinner.

GRACE: My bosom get in the way.

KENNETH: Then diet.

GRACE: I aren't goin' on a diet so you dun' ave to grease the combine.

KENNETH: Good a reason as any.

GRACE: And dun't forget the dance tomorrer night.

KENNETH: Tch!

GRACE: Lookin' forward to that.

KENNETH: The best field for pickin' mushrooms on my farm backs on to the airforce base.

GRACE: Be careful.

KENNETH: I tell you what I'll do. I'll keep my bedroom slippers on. It's a light dew and they won't get wet, and the Yanks will take me for what I am. A plain English farmer.

GRACE: Don't bank on it.

KENNETH: I'll be as long as it takes me to pick a grain pan full of mushrooms.

KENNETH *goes.* GRACE *sits. Music plays, then stops.* GRACE *looks at her watch.*

GRACE: He's late.

Music plays again. GRACE *uncrosses her legs and re-crosses them the other way. Music stops. She looks at her watch.*

GRACE: He's bin gone a day now. Twenty-four hours. I think I'm gettin' worried. Soon be time to make enquiries. Start askin' round a bit.

She goes. Music intro to FARMERS' *song.*

6   THE BODY

Part One

The FARMERS *of the parish, sing a song.*

FARMERS:
The farmers of this parish
Would dearly love to tell,
All about Mother May
A body and a – well,
Mother May went cocklin',
No, we haven't started right,
To get the yarn out viddy
We got to start the night
Before,
When Stanly stuck her bloomers
In the roof to stop the leak,
So she could take the bucket out
From underneath.
So now she got the *bucket*
To do with what she like,
And with the *bucket* in er 'and
She set sail on her bike.
Bike got a puncture
So she ayved'n in the ditch,
Decide to pick some cockles
From beneath the iron bridge.
Now *this* is where the story start,
With the cockles, and the *body*,
And Alice, and the iron bridge,
The bucket, and the . . .

> MRS MAY *and* ALICE *walking marchez sur place.* MRS MAY *muddy to the knee and carrying a bucket full of cockles.*

ALICE: Mornin' Mrs May.

MAY: Mornin' Alice.

ALICE: Hear the larks?

MAY: Lovely.

ALICE: You'm lookin' rosy Mrs May.

MAY: Thank you.

ALICE: Like you bin stridin' against the wind.

MAY: Bin over the cliff.

ALICE: You'm muddy half way to the knee.

MAY: Ah. Bin in the mud.

ALICE: And you have in your hand a bucket.

MAY: There now.

ALICE: Bin cocklin'?

MAY: Observant Alice.

ALICE: Bin under th'iron bridge?

MAY: Iron bridge Alice yes.

ALICE: Iron bridge is it?

MAY: And I've found more'n cockles.

ALICE: People often do, under th'iron bridge.

MAY: I was jabbin' about with me toes in the mud, jabbin' about for a cockle,

ALICE: Ez . . .

MAY: And me foot oozed on summin soft.

ALICE: Flesh.

MAY: I gived it a prod with me stick and it felt like Stanly's belly.

ALICE: Twad'n Stanly . . .

MAY: An' I put me 'and down, and twined me finger in a strand of seaweed.

ALICE: Hair . . .

MAY: 'Twas a body, what I found beneath th'iron bridge.

ALICE: Dead?

MAY: As a doormat.

> ALICE *stops to consider this and* MAY *stops also.*

ALICE: Still there is 'e?

MAY: I ab'm brung the bugger 'ome in the bucket.

ALICE: Just the one was it?

MAY: How many do 'e want?

ALICE: Better inform an authority ad'n'e?

MAY: I will do Alice, after I've 'ad me photograph took with it.

ALICE: 'Ere come Archie Gross. Inform 'e.

MAY: I dun't inform Archie Gross a nothin'. Me an' 'e dun't mix.

ALICE: Inform Gilbert. Policeman.

MAY: I will do Alice. But that there body belong to me. So dun't you go yakkin'.

> ARCHIE GROSS *walking marchez sur place. He carries an empty bucket.*

GROSS: Archie Gross, you're a lucky man. The sun's shinin' and the larks are singin'. You've an empty bucket in your 'and, danglin', by thy side, swingin' fore an' back in time with a loose and easy gait, which is step by step drawin' 'e closer to the cockle beds below the iron bridge. And there id'n nothin' like a bucket fulla cockles in the world, bar a good eggy tart like Tysie make. Aw. Cloud loomin' on the horizon, in the bulbous shape a Mrs May. She bring rain to me, she an' me dun't conglomerate. Look like she bin cocklin', so thass summin I d'know 'bout 'er. Less she knaw 'bout me less she can yack around the parish. And there's Alice with 'er, sprig a blossom brought out be the rain.

They converge.

Mornin' Mrs May.

MAY: So they say.

GROSS (*raising his hat*): Mornin' Alice.

ALICE: Mornin', Mr Gross.

GROSS: Hear the larks?

ALICE: Lovely.

GROSS: Bin for a jaunt?

MAY: There and back. Whass that bucket?

GROSS: Ohh, 'tis a bucket.

MAY: I noticed, you carry a bucket.

GROSS: I could say the same about you.

MAY: But I'm on me way back. You'm on your way.

GROSS: Ah. I'm er, goin' to milk the cow.

MAY: Out here?

GROSS: I have a cow, by name a Buttercup, who wander.

MAY: I hope she yield a good gallon.

They pass.

FARMERS (*sing*):
So off they went
To East and West
With little said
And love lost less
Mr Gross had told a fib,
Proper little whopper
Mrs May and Alice went
To winkle out a copper.

GILBERT *stands at the station desk. A pile of dollar bills and a box of popcorn sit on the desk-top.* GILBERT *eats popcorn. He closes the book and buttons up his jacket.* MAY *strides in followed by* ALICE.

GILBERT: Mornin' Mrs May.

MAY: Now thun.

GILBERT: Mornin' Alice.

ALICE: Mmmmmmmmmmmmmmmm.

MAY: Gilbert.

ALICE: Mmmmmmmmmm.

MAY: Gilbert.

GILBERT: Goin' dance tonight?

MAY: Got summin for 'e. Now listen 'ere boy . . .

ALICE: What dance?

GILBERT: Parish 'all.

ALICE: Dance tonight, is there?

MAY: Gilbert . . .

GILBERT: Goin'?

MAY: Gilbert . . .

ALICE: Mmmmmmm. Who's playin'?

GILBERT: Manny Cockle and the Big Four Combo.

ALICE: Ooh.

MAY: Gilbert!

ALICE: You gonna take me?

GILBERT: Mmmmmmmmm.

MAY: Christ!

ALICE: Cus I got to go now . . .

MAY: Alice will you stop yakkin' maid!

GILBERT: Where to?

ALICE: Eat me dinner.

MAY: Gilbert you on duty or no?

GILBERT: What 'e got for dinner?

MAY: GILBERT!

ALICE: Eggy tart.

　　ALICE *goes.*

MAY: *Now* thun!

GILBERT: Eh?

MAY: I found a dead body cocklin'.

GILBERT: Whass a dead body doin' cocklin'.

MAY: *I* was cocklin', the body was dead.

GILBERT: Where to?

8 THE BODY

MAY: Iron bridge.

GILBERT: Under'n?

MAY: Ez you, under'n.

GILBERT: Hell. Whose body is it?

MAY: I dunnaw. E'm washed up more like. Up the estuary, out the sea.

GILBERT: Aw.

MAY: You comin' or no?

GILBERT: I got 'ave me dinner.

MAY: Gaw damme boy 'twill be washed out again time you've 'ad your dinner!

GILBERT (*not enthusiastic*): Come on thun.

They go.

FARMERS (*sing*):
Gilbert was reluctant,
To say the very least,
To go and dig up bodies
Where bodies don't exist.
But before we carry on with them,
We've raced a bit ahead,
We must return to Mr Gross,
Who's *at* the cockle beds.

ARCHIE GROSS *cockling. He sits, removes his boots and rolls his trousers up. Checks the independence of his toes, walks a bit and whistles quietly to himself. Suddenly he plunges his foot into the mud, and feels for a cockle. Then he plunges his other foot, and he is cockling. He sings* . . .

GROSS: There is nothing like a cockle . . . We are poor black cockles, who have lost our way . . . Old man cockle . . . Cockles in the night . . . Red cockles in the sunset . . . Once, I had a secret cockle . . . 123 o'clock 4 o'clock cockle, 567 o'clock 8 o'clock cockle I'm gonna rock, around, the cockle tonight . . .

His foot action turns into the twist and he is carried away. Then he stops, his face changes, and he feels very carefully with his toes. He's found the BODY.

GROSS: Hell.

He starts to edge his feet horizontally along the BODY, *stopping at significant places. At last he gets to the head.*

Body.

He feels some more.

Dead. Damme. Now what. Shift'n. Handcart. Take'n church. Inform the rector.

GROSS *goes off. He leaves the* BODY *lying there. The* BODY *is covered from head to toe with mud.*

FARMERS (*sing*):
Now this is where our story start
To gather its momentum,
Mr Gross and handcart
Were there and back in no time.

GROSS *comes back with a handcart. He lifts the* BODY *on and off as they sing.*

The body lifted off the flats
And placed with haste
Upon the trap.
Mrs May, with rumblin' gait,
Arrived with Gilbert,
A mite too late.

MRS MAY *and* GILBERT *arrive on the scene, panting. She looks around her, conducts the proceedings like a military exercise.*

MAY: Take your boots and stockin's off boy.

GILBERT: Eh?

She hitches her skirts and plunges her foot in the mud.

MAY: Plunge your foot in.

GILBERT: Eh?

MAY: Got 'ome 'twas rainin'. Said to Stanly, 'Where's me bloomers?' 'E said, 'Stoppin' up the leak in the roof.' I said, 'Proper job, cockles for tea.' Plunge your foot in boy.

She plunges her other foot.

This is the spot. He'm down 'ere.

She feels about. No BODY.

Damme e'm sunk.

GILBERT: Eh?

MAY: Take your trousers off boy.

GILBERT (*taking off his trousers*): Eh?

MAY: 'E've gone deep. 'Ave to probe a bit.

GILBERT: Who's the policeman around 'ere.

MAY: *There* now.

GILBERT: What now?

MAY: That there body . . . 's vanished.

GILBERT: Gyat. Twad'n never there. 'Tis a figment.

MAY: Praise the lord! E'm a Lazarus! E've took up his bed an' walked! Advance with me Gilbert! To the rector!

And she's gone. GILBERT *picks up his trousers and follows.* ARCHIE GROSS, *pulling his hand cart.*

FARMERS (*sing*):
With flying skirt
And rolling lurch
She forged a path
Toward the church
With Gilbert, close behind.
Over hill
And down the dip,
Archie Gross
Cracked his whip
And galloped with his find.

GROSS: Archie Gross, you'm a lucky man. You set out this mornin' with nothin' more in mind 'n' a handsome bucket fulla cockles, and here y'are returnin' 'ome with a cartload a dead body! Hero a the parish! I'll have 'em all yakkin'. An' Mrs May steamin' like a silage pit for lettin' a dead body through her toes while jabbin' for a cockle beneath the iron bridge. She think she'm the big I am, but who found the body!

The BODY *slips off the back of the cart.*

FARMERS (*sing*):
No sooner had he said those words,
He reached an incline in the road,
Steeper steeper climbed the cart,
And the body slipped off onto the path.

The church. The RECTOR *stands by the lych gate dressed as a Chinaman.* ARCHIE *arrives with his empty cart.*

ARCHIE: Rector! I see you're dressed as a Chinaman.

RECTOR: Observant Archie.

ARCHIE: And the church seem somewhat altered.

RECTOR: On the outside.

ARCHIE: Now thun.

RECTOR: The nave is exactly as you might remember it.

ARCHIE: Got summin show 'e.

RECTOR: You see Archie it started with the fund raisin'.

ARCHIE: Twad'n me who stripped the lead off the steeple.

RECTOR: No 'twas the October gale.

ARCHIE: I lost a dutch barn in that one . . . now look 'ere look, in the 'and cart . . .

RECTOR: I said to Jack Steeple the steeplejack that steeple, Jack, is leakin'. Jack Steeple looked at me and then 'e eyed the steeple. Rector, said Jack, the leak in that steeple is gonna take some stoppin'. That steeple's bent. I could erect a pagoda cheaper. A pagoda said I. Aye said Jack. A pagoda. I looked at Jack, then I eyed the steeple. All the while my 'and clasped the forty seb'm an' sixpence, the parish response to my appeal, includin' bingo, and I said to meself, so Jack couldn' 'ear, nuts. For all the attention I get on a Sunday mornin' I might as well be a Chinaman, so here I am, pagoda, Chinese cassock wi' dragons on, and pointed hat. And do you know Archie? You're the first bugger who's noticed.

ARCHIE: Then rector 'tis your lucky day. There's a body in the back a that cart!

RECTOR: Lead me to it!

ARCHIE: Follow.

ARCHIE *leads the* RECTOR *round to the back of the cart. The cart is empty.*

Aw. Aw my gor.

RECTOR: Dearodear.

ARCHIE: I tell 'e Rector 'e was 'ere! Dead as a doormat, lyin' in the back a the cart!

RECTOR: Come inside the pagoda Archie, an' I'll relieve 'e of a sin or two, you'm clearly in need of spiritual aid.

GROSS: 'Tis Mrs May. She'm a witch.

RECTOR: Mrs May is a stalwart of the parish.

GROSS: She'll stop a pig bleedin' a mile off, I seed 'er do it!

RECTOR: She has a shiny pew, through constant use Archie, I'm surprised you found your way here.

GROSS: She spirited the bugger off the cart, set the parish yakkin'!

RECTOR: 'Tis a sad state Archie when a man come to blaspheme in the shadow of the house of er, God.

GROSS: 'Tis a damn sorry state when a man can't go cocklin', find a dead body, an' call the bugger 'is own!

He strides off. RECTOR *goes off.*

MAY *and* GILBERT, *striding sur place.*

MAY: Stride out Gilbert! We got a sensation on our hands! God look kindly upon they who shine hisnpews and I'm goin' meet this Lazarus, in the flesh, wi' blood pumpin' through!

ARCHIE GROSS *striding towards them.*

GROSS: Archie Gross, you'm a misunderstood man. If I could wrench the rector away from 'is rice wine I could show'n a thing or two make 'is Chinese cassock curl.

MAY: Head for the church Gilbert! The steeple glowin' with a strange an' eerie light. E'm in there yarnin' with the rector more like.

GILBERT: With a gallon a rice wine.

GROSS: This is a case for the p'lice. Gilbert got 'ear 'bout this.

MAY: That there Archie Gross, dun't knaw what e'm missin', milkin', I'll set the parish yakkin', shove'n out the limelight.

GROSS: Mother May, blind as a badger, couldn' see a dead body if 'e stood up an' looked 'er in the face, got to resort to witchcraft get 'old of 'er dead bodies . . .

MAY: There's one or two points I want to raise with this Lazarus, 'bout Moses an' the locusts.

GROSS: That there rector id'n no good. I was churchwarden there three years an 'e thought I was me brother.

MAY, GILBERT *and* GROSS *all converge on the* BODY *from different directions.*

MAY (*seeing the* BODY): *There* now!

GROSS: Hah! WHERE D'Y GET THAT BODY TO!

MAY: That there's MY BODY!

GROSS: YOUR BODY IS IT! And WHAT make 'e so cocky on THAT ONE?

MAY: Cos I FOUND of 'er!

GROSS: THEN WE HAVE A DISPUTE ON OUR HANDS!

MAY: Why's THAT?

GROSS: Cos *I* found of 'er!

MAY: Milkin' cows?

GROSS: I wad'n milkin' no cow, so there's the first eye-opener!

MAY: Then you'm a dirty liard!

GROSS: I'm a stalwart of the parish!

MAY: An' I'm a pillar of the church!

GROSS: Then go an' 'old the roof up!

MAY: No roof left, lead you've pinched!

GROSS: Well you'll always find a willin' pair a bloomers, for to stop up the leaks!

MAY: That was Stanly! Gilbert! Arbitrate!

GILBERT: I'm gonna notify an authority.

GROSS: Which authority?

GILBERT: Dunnaw. Water board's nearest.

MAY: You idn' gonna notify no bugger 'til we got this body sorted out who it belongs to an' I've 'ad me picture took with it on the parish 'all steps!

ARCHIE: Who it belong to is perfectly plain, who dug'n up and brung'n ere?

GILBERT: You did Arch.

MAY: Who's foot first found flesh!?

GILBERT: Yours Mrs May.

MAY: Then I demand the right, to be photographed, on the parish 'all steps, with this 'ere body propped up alongside, exclusive, black and white across the nation's news-stands!

GROSS: Over my dead body!

MAY: Archie Gross you'm a greedy grabbin' man. Defeat stands 'ere, starin' y'in the face, and still your fingers spread and close like talons graspin' air. No man hath less deserved notoriety and no man seeks it more. If this body could speak. If this mouth could utter but one sentence more before his passage through the endless night he would raise his bloodless hand, point to me, and say . . .

GILBERT: Thass goodbye to me dinner me brother's et it now.

MAY: . . . I belong to Mrs May. What further proof do 'e need.

GROSS: You expect me to dribble? She've 'ad the whole parish dribblin' before now but not me. Archie Gross dun't dribble!

GILBERT: Steak an' kidney bloody puddin' down me brother's gullet. E'm fatter'n a young shag and 'ere's me thinner'n wind an' 'ungry.

MAY: Dry mouths dun't dribble Archie Gross I knaw that. Snakes' tongues flick and no saliva oils their jaw!

GROSS: Well. Well. Now we knaw how far we'm prepared to go.

GILBERT: She got to callin' y'a snake yet Archie?

GROSS: Yes. That last one. Snake.

GILBERT: Right. That wraps it up. Satisfied Mrs May?

MAY: Archie Gross. Call this body mine.

GILBERT (*spreads his hands*): No mercy.

GROSS: Your foot found flesh first. My foot fell on tainted skin.

GILBERT: Nicely put Arch. Lost on the old bat but I could see the dignity in it. I'm arrestin' this body.

MAY: What!?

GROSS: Hell!

GILBERT (*to the* BODY): Anything you say will be taken down an' used against you in evidence. I hope you gotta passport.

They all look at the BODY. *It keeps its mouth shut.*

Unless anyone's prepared to raise bail . . .

They have no money about them.

I'll put me trousers on, go an' get me Lambretta, an' run'n down the lock up.

MAY: 'Ad your dinner yet Gilbert?

GILBERT: No.

MAY: Then 'ere's a bucket a cockles.

GILBERT: Aw. Ta.

MAY: Bail.

GILBERT: Hell! I'm hungry. Hungry as a gap in the hedge. Bucket a cockles a go down well. Bloody job to keep a dead body upright on the back of a Lambretta . . .

MAY: Thass settled that thun.

GROSS: Vanity and greed win the day.

MAY: I'll go an' get me 'air done now. Phone Reuter, should get the world's press 'ere by four a clock.

She takes the BODY *and makes for home, the* BODY *across her shoulder.*
GILBERT *pulls his trousers on. The* RECTOR *appears. He's been running.*

RECTOR: Ah. Caught up with 'e at last.

GROSS: Too late, the bird 'ave flown.

RECTOR: I gather there's a body for me Gilbert.

GROSS: This idiot 'ad the bugger under arrest. Some bloody p'liceman you are, let a dead body slip out your 'ands.

GILBERT: I'm that 'ungry I could eat these cockles raw. Shell's'n all. Oo are you?

RECTOR: Rector.

GILBERT: Whass this Chinese rigout?

RECTOR: Like it?

GILBERT: It make a splash.

GROSS: Fower time she done the dirty on me. Clodploddin' bastard farmers in this parish is near bankrupt tryin' keep up wi' me. She snatch a body from me an' I'll snatch that body back an' I'll paint my body black to get my body back cus that body's *my* body more'n tis anybody's, s'much as this body's my body so what better way to get a body eh?

GILBERT: Eh?

RECTOR: You talkin' 'bout the body?

GROSS: Yes.

RECTOR: That body deserve a Christian burial Archie. No plottin'. I want that body clean an' greased and laid out in the vestry before evensong.

GROSS: I'll tell 'e summin Rector. I'm a key figure in this parish. King pin. I'm the man they look to, and after lookin', follow. I aren't used to bein' shoved this way an' that and bein' made a damn fool of. You want that body you'll 'ave to stand in line, cus the battle id'n over yet!

THE BODY

He stalks off.

RECTOR: Tell 'e summin Gilbert. I gotta feelin' the clergy ab'm got the status in the parish no more. Worship seem to me to be very much a byline.

GILBERT: Rector is it?

RECTOR: There's few who bother to make the journey up the hill to the pagoda, and them as do dun't listen.

GILBERT: Got your passport?

RECTOR: And of course, that makes my life . . .

GILBERT: Whass it like in China?

RECTOR: . . . very, very, lonely.

The RECTOR wanders off.

GILBERT: Hm.

He fishes a notebook from somewhere and writes a memo. Then he picks up the bucket and goes.

FARMERS (*sing*):
Back at home
Grace had
Waited
Long enough
For Kenneth to return.

GRACE sits at home.

GRACE: Better go out lookin' for 'im. I better tell 'em I miss'n. Cus I do. Though I can't be sure. If they say do you miss'n, course I a say yes. Dun't she lub'm? Course I lub'm. Well. I miss'n. I lub'm, cus 'e's there. But if I was honest, would I say I lub'm cus I miss'n, or I lub'm cus 'e's there, or what? I'm on me own see. If I'm on me own I worry. In this 'ouse on this des'late farm in the dark nights. Do I worry cus I lub'm? Or cus I'm on me own? Then there's the dance. 'E's gotta be back for that. I better go an' look for'n.

She goes off.

FARMERS (*sing*):
A day, a night,
And half another
Passed
Before she went
And asked
Her Mother
To offer
Her advice.

GRACE *on. Her* MOTHER *upstage, bending, taking eggy tart from the oven, back to the audience.*

MOTHER: Dun't bother me.

GRACE *walks down stage.* MOTHER *off.*

GILBERT *in the station. He eats a fairy cake.* GRACE *walks in.*

GRACE: Gilbert. Kenneth's missin'.

GILBERT: One bloody fairy cake.

GRACE: I asked Mother, and she was sympathetic, but she said the first thing I should do is report it to you.

GILBERT: Whass she doin', Mother?

GRACE: Smelt like eggy tart.

GILBERT *shuts up shop and puts his tunic on as* GRACE *talks.*

He went out pickin' mushrooms yesterday mornin' an' e ab'm come back. I aren't sure what I'm thinkin' . . . You comin' to look for'n?

GILBERT: I'm goin' 'ave me bloody dinner.

GRACE: Aw c'mon . . .

GILBERT: Dun't bother me . . .

He goes off. GRACE *turns to the three* FARMERS, *who are discussing in a circle.*

GRACE: Excuse me . . .

FARMER ONE: Whose sheep was it?

FARMER TWO: Mine.

FARMER THREE: Whose field was it?

FARMER ONE: Mine.

FARMER TWO: And whose fence was it?

FARMER THREE: Mine.

GRACE: Excuse me . . .

FARMERS (*pointing at each other*): So your sheep was in 'is field when 'e broke down your fence . . .

GRACE: Er . . .

FARMERS: Yup.

GRACE: Oy!

FARMERS: We are meeting to discuss.

GRACE: Kenneth's missin'.

FARMERS: Dun't bother we . . .

ARCHIE GROSS *on.*

So what we'm 'ere to debate, is who pay for the fence. . .

They notice ARCHIE GROSS *and stop talking. He approaches them and they ignore him, walk off. He glowers.*

GRACE (*in tears*): Archie, Kenneth went pickin' mushrooms an' 'e never come back. I dunno what I'm feeling. No one seem that concerned. I thought you, bein' 'is father, thought you might juss worry with me, juss worry a li'l bit. 'E's disappeared, dun't you care? 'E's vanished! I knaw 'e's slow on the uptake Arch I knaw, an' often I've 'eard you say 'e id'n worthy a the name a Gross, and indicated doubt at his ability to produce a progeny for to carry on the line but 'e got a sweet nature Arch, we a git there one day, we'll 'ave a li'l boy, li'l grandson for 'e, li'l, perky chap, but I gotta find 'im first! Please Arch, please . . .

ARCHIE GROSS, *who has been buried in thought, turns on* GRACE.

GROSS: Heed this Grace . . .

GRACE: Yes?

GROSS: Tomorrer night the name of Gross shall scorch its path across the sky and light this parish from Winnards Perch to Rumford with a neon power!

GRACE: Oh . . .

GROSS: And in a forgotten des'late field, 'neath a dark hedge shadow creepin', on her belly, shall Mother May slide, and eat grass. The taste of nettle sweet her tongue and revenge ride upon her back!

GRACE: Please help me please . . .

GROSS: Dun't bother me! (*He's off.*)

The FARMERS *sing, in a dramatic, operatic way, with descant, as* MRS MAY *makes her grand, sweeping entrance, the following aria:*

FARMERS (*sing*):
The very next day
Mrs May
Had her photo
In the papers.
The world's press
On the parish hall steps
Had snapped a legend
In the making.
Famous now, notorious,
And Archie Gross was furious . . .

MRS MAY *and* ALICE *sit on the parish hall steps.* GROSS *slinks on and glowers in the background.* MAY *and* ALICE *have a pile of newspapers before them and are eagerly leafing through them. As the scene progresses,* FARMERS *wander on and warmly greet* MRS MAY *as if she's a celebrity, they maintain a discreet distance, at the same time interested in what is going on.*

MAY: See that there look?

ALICE: Is that you?

MAY: No thass the body. I got me bonnet on.

ALICE: They got a good angle there.

MAY: Thass the *Daily Mirror*. They took that from behind.

FARMER: Morning Mrs May.

MAY (*to* ALICE): First time 'e've spoke to me since nineteen forty-six. The best one's in the *Daily Telegraph* . . . (*Raising her voice a bit.*) Opposite the court and social. Captured me square on in the foreground with the sun behind and the body in sharp relief.

ALICE: Oh yes, that's very plain. Very clear and sharp.

FARMER: Oho Mrs May . . .

MAY (*under her breath*): Gittome.

The RECTOR *comes on. He notices* MAY, *and then* ARCHIE. *He has in his hand a bible. He takes a stance on the steps.*

Tid'n too grainy. The body's come out nice. You can see 'tis a body, and you can see 'tis dead. There's no mistakin' thass a dead body see?

ALICE: Thass dead all right.

MAY: Queen'll see that photograph.

ALICE: Will 'er?

FARMER: How do you do Mrs May?

MAY: That was Stanly. She look in the

court and social and see what she'm doin' for the day.

ALICE: Hell. Where's the body to now?

MAY: Up 'ome. On the couch, in the parlour.

ALICE: Dunne stink?

MAY: Couldn' say. I aren't that nasal.

They bury themselves in their papers. The FARMERS *slowly edge over and look over their shoulders without them noticing. The* RECTOR *starts to preach.*

RECTOR: Citizens! Congregation! I have come down, from my pagoda, on the hill, this afternoon, to preach a sermon in the forum, as it were. I speak, from the heart, of the parish! I have an important somethin' to say to you all. Please, I beg your ears hear what your Rector has to say . . .

FARMER: Thass a very flatterin' picture in *The Times* Mrs May, if I may venture my opinion.

FARMER: Definitely dead innit.

RECTOR: . . . An event has come to pass, which, bein' Rector, of course I was one of the first informed. Now, as you probably all know, I'm talkin' about the body. This body has bin passed from pillar to post, shoved this way and that without so much as a prayer bein' offered up in his presence. There are people in this parish, who are usin' this 'ere body for their own ends. To further their own notoriety. Squabbles have broken out amongst respected members of the community over some poor chap who's dead. Even now I'm told he is lying on a couch in a private house! This is repugnant behaviour, thought of as lowly even by ants! I'm here this afternoon to uphold the standards laid down by the church, and ask those responsible for this appalling sin, to repent and bring the body to me!

GRACE *comes on.*

GRACE: Rector . . .

RECTOR: Aww what?

GRACE: Y'ab'm seed Kenneth?

RECTOR: Oh, piss off . . .

GRACE *wanders down and joins the poring crowd.*

People!

No one takes any notice of the RECTOR. *He starts to speak in Chinese. Slowly, as he speaks, people hear what he's saying and turn and listen. Towards the end of his speech, everybody is listening to the* RECTOR *speaking in Chinese, and* GILBERT *wanders on.*

GILBERT: Whass goin on?

RECTOR (*continues to speak in Chinese*).

GILBERT: Who is this man?

ALICE (*vehemently*): Bloody Chinaman, blind?

GILBERT: Now thun mister. Less see your passport!

RECTOR (*continues to speak in Chinese*).

GILBERT *takes the* RECTOR *roughly by the arm.*

GILBERT: Come on skipper. We got some cross examinin' to be done . . .

GILBERT *manhandles the confused* RECTOR *off. The* FARMERS *come forward to speak while* MRS MAY *and* GROSS *clear off,* ALICE *remains seated on the step and* GRACE *sits beside her, studying closely the paper that is left.*

FARMERS (*speak*):
We, the farmers of this parish,
Uphold the moral standards
Set down by the church,
As rooted in the land
As the sugar beet we nurture
And unchanged by events
That happen round us,
We remain entrenched
In the ditches of
Our opinion.
Nothing sways us.
What we think is what we do,
From market day to
Milking time,
What we see and who
We meet are liable to
The same fogbound horizons
Framed by the seasons,
And regular as the lessons
Read from the bible.

The FARMERS *move upstage whilst* ALICE *speaks to* GRACE.

ALICE: I said to Gilbert, 'Why d'y wanna wear your uniform to the dance,' I said, 'Wear that tweed jacket you wore to the hunt ball!'. 'E said 'e like wearin' 'is uniform. I said, 'What is it to be your uniform or me? I aren't goin' no fuckin' dance with a policeman. I wanna go dance wi' Gilbert . . .'

GRACE: . . . So y'ab'm seed'n thun.

ALICE: . . . Gilbert said, 'I am my uniform,' I said, 'I'll go dance wi' Benny.' 'E said, 'Benny's a twit.' I said, 'Not 'alf as big a fuckin' twit as you.' 'E said, 'If you go dance wi' Benny I'll arrest the bugger.' I said, 'You arrest Benny I'll smack y'in the fuckin' mouth.' 'E said, 'You smack me in the fuckin' mouth.' So I smacked'n in the mouth an 'e arrested me an' asked me for me passport so I said, 'Now what you gonna do Mr fuckin' Chief Constable . . .?'

GRACE: This body id'n Kenneth, tis too square-shouldered.

ALICE: . . . 'E said, 'I'm gonna take 'e down the station an' lock 'e up for the night.' I said, 'Aww Mr Powerful I inna fraida you an' your fuckin' uniform. You take 'at uniform off,' I said, 'an' put your tweed jacket on see if you got the fuckin' guts to lock me up . . .'

GRACE: You're sure you ab'm . . .

ALICE: So off come the uniform and on go the tweed jacket an 'e's standin' there lookin' bloody sheepish rubbin' 'is gob where I gib'm a smack an' I says, 'Come on thun.' 'E says, 'Where we goin'?' I said, 'Dance.' 'E said, 'Aw all right thun.' So off we went dancin', soon as we got there there was fuckin' Mavis Rickeard all dolled up in 'er bandy legs'n mini skirt an' 'e couldn' keep 'is eyes off 'er so 'e danced wi' she an' I danced wi' Benny . . .

GRACE: And that was the end of that!

GRACE and ALICE remain seated. The FARMERS of the parish start to speak. They are joined throughout by members of the parish, as indicated, until by the end everyone is speaking, backed by music, swelling to a crescendo. When the RECTOR joins, he is elevated from behind so he is above the others, handcuffed.

FARMERS:
In the days before the binder
They cut it with a scythe,
By Christ it made your back ache
And that can't be denied.
Then along came the tractor
And a reaper with a blade,
It cut the job in half,
Backs and labour saved . . .

ALICE (*joins*):
But the old men shook their heads,
Wrung arthritic hands,
Rolled bloodshot eyes
Toward the skies
And prophetically sighed

GROSS (*joins*):
'Tis too easy for 'em now,
They'll invent machines
To milk a cow
Before the decade's out,
And then where will they be?

GILBERT (*joins*):
Sittin' in the devil's lap,
Drinkin' from the devil's tap,
Waitin' for the next invention,
Surely not our Lord's intention.
But true enough we sat around,
Ragwort spread across the ground,
Waiting for the magic sound

MAY (*joins*):
The massive, marching devil's son,
With eight four cut, threshing drum,
And bagging shute, all in one,
Climb the ladder, take the wheel,
Start the motor, devastate a whole
Eight acre field
In a single dusty day,
One man sat upon
A raging rattlin' metal movin'
Mountain, the leviathan
Has come!

The old men shook their heads,
Laughed at this invention,
Wrung arthritic hands,
Rolled bloodshot eyes
Toward the skies
And somehow knew that intervention
This time, was divine.
So preposterous, so sublimely wicked
Was this fruit of Satan's union
With avaracious Croesus.
True enough, they cocked their ears,
Listening for the voice of Jesus,
Waiting to be warned that life
Can't be easy.
Somewhere round the corner,
Payment for this monster –
In the shape of aching back,
Broken finger, lack of sleep

Through skin peeled feet lurked
With sharpened scythe to reap
Our ease and happiness on earth.
RECTOR (*joins*):
Not long they prayed
Before their prophecy
Was heeded by an angered God.
No more, said he, pointing with
Arthritic finger,
Looking down with bloodshot eyes
And wrathy thirst for vengeance
Boomed with thunderous voice
RECTOR (*solo, with booming voice, pointing with manacled hands at* GRACE *huddled down stage*):
BEFORE YOU EVER MAKE THIS
COMBINE WORK
BY CHRIST YOU GOT TO
GREASE THE BUGGER FIRST!

Music stops. They all disperse to reveal a fifty gallon drum full of mud centre stage.

ARCHIE GROSS's *farm.* GROSS *undresses before the drum, down to his underpants. Doves coo. At the back of the stage* GILBERT *enters on his Lambretta. A Pan Am bag is strapped on and from his belt dangles a menacing bunch of handcuffs.*

GILBERT: Oy!

GROSS: What?

    GILBERT *indicates the pillion seat of the Lambretta.*

GILBERT: 'Op on!

GROSS: Uh?

GILBERT: Arrest. Passport?

GROSS: 'For?

GILBERT: 'Fficial!

GROSS: Gittome!

GILBERT: C'mon!

GROSS: I'm busy!

GILBERT: Same 'ere!

GROSS: Then sling your 'ook!

    GILBERT *alights from his Lambretta and approaches* GROSS.

GILBERT: Come on Archie I got the 'ole parish to round up.

GROSS: 'Ole parish?

GILBERT: Yeah.

GROSS: Why?

GILBERT: Can't divulge.

GROSS: Why?

GILBERT: 'Tis official.

GROSS: Body?

GILBERT: What body?

GROSS: What body *the* body *my* body!

GILBERT: Dunnaw what you're talkin 'bout skipper.

GROSS: Oh, course, 'tis official now. 'Ad a rocket up 'is ass an' now 'e's in the shit. You piss off 'ome 'fore I tell your mother, I got business to conduct!

GILBERT: Aw dun't tell Mother for chrissake.

GROSS: Three days ago Gilbert, 'eads turned when I bid at market. Noses twitched an' brains started tickin'. When I strode forth with an empty bucket in me 'and speculation rose like steam from a fresh laid cowpat as to that bucket's fate. An' I didn' let 'em down. I found a dead body, cocklin'. I swaggered back with it, proud man, but oh, how the mighty have fallen. For three days I've carried round in my head nothin' more'n a janglin' mix of humiliation and revenge. But I had a plan, and now that plan is goin' into action, and no 'andcuff danglin' copper's goona stop its glorious journey till once again this parish doffs its hat to me!

GILBERT: Bullshit! Doff your ass on the back a that Lambretta Buster! Pronto!

GROSS *leaps into the drum of mud and submerges himself completely. He emerges covered in mud.*

GROSS: Do your business thun.

    GILBERT *is taken aback.*

GILBERT: Hell.

    GROSS *re-submerges for another coat.* GRACE *arrives.*

GILBERT: Ah!

GRACE: What?

GILBERT: C'mon the Lambretta.

GRACE: You id'n arrestin' me I'm your bloody sister!

PART ONE

GILBERT: Aw please Gracy . . .

GRACE: Gittout of it 'fore I tell Mother . . .

GILBERT: Aw, tch!

GRACE: Where's Archie?

GILBERT: In there.

He indicates the drum and goes. GROSS *re-emerges.*

GRACE: That you Archie?

GROSS: Ah. Grace. Give us 'and wi' this . . .

GROSS *trundles the drum off. The* FARMERS *lurk, perhaps lend an unobtrusive hand.*

GRACE: Archie. Kenneth's gone missin'.

GROSS: Gonna give Mother May the fright of 'er life . . .

GRACE: 'Tis the yank marines only normally as you know they only keep'n till dinnertime . . .

GROSS: Need the parish there, bear witness . . .

GRACE: Only 'e went off without greasin' the combine, an' I need 'elp, greasin' it . . .

GROSS: Outside 'er parlour window.

GRACE: An' I need to git that out the way Arch . . .

GROSS *stops in his tracks.*

GROSS: WHAT!

GRACE: See?

GROSS: Kenneth. 'E've gone you say?

GRACE: 'E ab'm bin 'ome for three days . . .

GROSS: AN 'E AB'M GREASED THE COMBINE!

GRACE: No, but . . .

GROSS: MY CHRIST ALMIGHTY! THAT BLOODY SON A MINE!

GRACE: Eh?

GROSS (*indicates the* FARMERS): WHAT THE HELL ARE THE PEOPLE A THIS PARISH GONNA SAY WHEN THEY HEAR THAT KENNETH GROSS, SON OF ARCHIE, HAS BUGGERED OFF AND LEFT HIS WIFE GRACE TO GREASE THE COMBINE!

GRACE: Well. Exactly.

GROSS: HAVEN'T THEY DONE ENOUGH TO ME!

GRACE: I bin all round the parish an' I've 'eard several innuendoes . . .

FARMERS (*severally*): Innuendo innuendo innuendo . . .

GROSS: I'LL BET YOU HAVE!

GRACE: What we gonna do?

GROSS: Be outside Mother May's at eight o'clock tonight. Sit outside 'er parlour window an' scream like a cat at exactly ten past.

GRACE: Eight.

GROSS: You got'n. Bring Gilbert if 'e've 'ad 'is dinner. Anyone else you can pressgang. After that we a' go on a search for that bastard wayward son a mine. Teach the bugger to GREASE THE COMBINE . . !

GRACE: Good job!

They go off, leaving the space empty.

ALICE *sits doing her needlepoint.* GILBERT *enters.*

ALICE: What you come for? Slap or tickle?

GILBERT: Now look 'ere. You're under arrest. Where's you're passport?

ALICE: Aww, not that again . . .

GILBERT: No this . . .

ALICE: Wouldn' say boo to a goose in 'is tweed jacket an' soon as 'e put 'is tunic on again 'e's back arrestin' me . . .

GILBERT: This is bloody serious this is . . .

ALICE: What is?

GILBERT: Can't divulge . . .

ALICE: You was divulgin' enough round the back a the parish 'all last night.

GILBERT: Uh?

ALICE: Wi' Mavis Rickeard. I was there when Benny switched 'is 'eadlights on, 'long with 'alf the district. You bin sid more round 'ere lately without trousers'n wid.

GILBERT: Aw 'ell . . .

ALICE: Benny said 'e wished 'e 'ad 'is airgun wid'n 'e woulda popped 'e right'n the ass . . .

GILBERT: Mother wad'n there was 'er?

ALICE: You woulda knawed soon enough.

GILBERT: I dunnaw sometimes she keep these things secret an' spring 'em on me at a later date. Ab'm told 'er 'ave 'e?

ALICE: Bloody will if y'arrest me. Oo've 'e brung in so far?

GILBERT: No one. 'Cept the Chinaman.

ALICE: Id'n doin' too well then are 'e. Whass up, id'n they payin' 'e enough?

GILBERT *sits close to* ALICE, *despondent. The handcuffs are between them so he places them on* ALICE's *lap.*

GILBERT: I got the feelin' the constabulary ab'm got the status in the parish no more. There's too much afoot. There's ancient rivalries blowin' up an' runnin' amok amongst the morals a the place. There's the Chinaman runnin' round pervertin' every bugger to Communism, there's the boys up the camp makin' impossible demands, payin' me all this money, an' 'ere's me catched bang in the middle, 'tis like a whirlpool, an' a course it go straight to me stomach . . .

ALICE: Come near me thun . . .

GILBERT: I gotta Pan Am bag fulla dollar bills I gotta pay Mrs May for the body . . .

ALICE: Pan Am bag you say?

GILBERT: Down the lock up yeah . . .

ALICE: Full you say?

GILBERT: Bulgin'.

ALICE: Thass 'ell of a lotta money.

GILBERT: Tis yeah . . .

ALICE: Aww, Gilbert. Darlin' . . .

GILBERT: I shouldna divulged it reely. Start with a tweed jacket well a tweed jacket what the 'ell (*Close to tears.*) twad'n my damn fault I weared a tweed jacket thass what they'm there for, balls an' parish 'all do's an' that, tweed jackets every bugger 'ad a tweed jacket an' where do it all lead to, arrest every bugger well thass a damn sight easier'n it look mister with me sister near distraction me mother lurkin' with 'er threats an' last night's eggy tart thrust across the table . . . tis . . . tis . . . if I could only git 'em all in one place . . . (*Sobbing now.*) with their trousers down, all lined up with their 'ands behind their backs I could snap snap snappetty snap 'em all up but where's the chance a that? 'Tis too much to ask Alice . . .

ALICE: Aww, darlin'.

GILBERT: All outside a winder, lookin' in a room, thass what I need . . .

ALICE: 'Tis the respect innit, whass lost . . .

GILBERT: I'm like a reckless rat. All me body's twitchin' . . .

ALICE: Respect an' love an' just a feelin' a bein' wanted. Needed by people, like your mother see she was never that maternal wi' you an' Grace, they all said that, she was cold towards you when she was carryin' Grace an' 'tis the rejection innit, aww, darlin'. An' I bin blind to it see.

GILBERT: Bloody blind.

ALICE: 'Tis all, duty. No, dotage. Aww, darlin' . . .

GILBERT: I'd love a li'l tickle.

ALICE: Would 'e? Where?

GILBERT: Just 'ere. Below me two-way radio.

ALICE: Aw dearest yes I give 'e li'l tickle . . .

GILBERT: Then I a carry on arrestin' . . .

ALICE: No 'urry sweet'eart . . .

GILBERT: I *gotta* do me duty see. 'Tis ingrained in me.

ALICE: Forget your duty. Live a bit. Less 'ave a tickle, we a still be 'ere tomorrer, live for now darlin', forget tomorrer, tomorrer's another day . . .

GRACE *tickles* GILBERT *and he laughs uncontrollably. They get to the point where it might develop into something else when* GRACE *enters.*

GRACE: GILBERT!

GILBERT (*hoisting his trousers up*): Aw Christ dun't tell mother . . .

GRACE: Gilbert, Kenneth's run off an' left

me to grease the combine . . .

GILBERT: WHAT! Stay 'ere Alice this is a job for the p'lice . . .

GRACE: An' Archie's gone up Mother May's . . . needs the parish as witness . . .

GILBERT: Never mind that we gotta . . . (?) . . . what?

GRACE: Gotta be outside 'er winder at eight o'clock.

GILBERT: That a do me. Foller!

They go off. The FARMERS *of the parish conclude their debate.*

FARMERS (*pointing to each other*): So you pay half towards the fence, if you give me two thirds of the fleece.

GRACE *rushes in.*

GRACE: Kenneth's run off an' left me to grease the combine!

GILBERT *and* ALICE *follow.*

Follow me men!

GILBERT, ALICE, GRACE *and the* FARMERS *of the parish walk in a line marchez sur place. They are in a hurry.*

GILBERT: I'm 'ungry. Oo gotta Nuttall's Minto?

FARMERS: I 'ave.

They each take a Nuttall's Minto from their pockets and pass it up the line.

ALICE: Can't see why you married a Gross Grace, they're none of 'em good.

GRACE: Kenneth's all right. 'E's an open book thass all.

FARMERS: What about the Rector? Oughta rope 'e in . . .

GILBERT: What rector?

ALICE: Gilbert dun't go church.

FARMERS: The one who dress like a Chinaman.

GILBERT: Thass a Chinaman.

FARMERS: Where's 'e to?

GILBERT: Arrested. Under interrogation. Anyone 'ere speak Chinese?

Silence.

Aw.

FARMERS: Where be us goin? Grease the combine?

GILBERT: Mother May's.

FARMERS: Aw.

They go off.

Revealed is MOTHER MAY's *parlour. A settee and two armchairs, facing out, arranged around a television, with its back to the audience. A window at the back.* MAY *sits on an armchair, then there's the settee in the middle with the* BODY *on it.* STANLY *is slouched in the other armchair, asleep with the cat on his lap. He wears a gasmask.*

MAY (*to the* BODY): This 'ere's my favourite programme. Comin' up. Stanly! Stanly. Favourite programme Stanly. Damme Stanly waky waky. Darlin' . . . Soon as 'e come 'ome 'e gather up the cat, fall in the chair an' nod off. Ab'm wavered for forty year. I aren't gonna git up out me seat'n rouse'n. Dun't git thanked f'rit. 'Swhy 'tis so nice t'ave someone to talk to for a change. 'E a wake up, when 'tis all over, there a be ructions, I a stampede upstairs to bed an' 'e a knock off back to sleep again till the cold wake'n up when the fire go out. An thass the way we d'go on. I dun't knit see. Aw. Kettle's boilin'.

She goes off into the kitchen. The window opens and GROSS *climbs through. He goes to the settee and removes the* BODY. *He takes it out the back, through another door, to the toilet and returns. He takes the cat from* STANLY's *knee and viciously wrings its neck. He replaces it on* STANLY's *knee. Then he sits on the settee where the* BODY *was.* GILBERT's *and* ALICE's *faces appear at the window.* MAY *returns with one cup of tea and a bun.*

Used to bring'n 'is tea in but the bugger never drunk it.

She places the tea and the bun on the sofa beside GROSS *and leans forward to watch the favourite programme.* GROSS *takes the bun and passes it back over the sofa to* GILBERT *whose hand is outstretched through the open window.* GILBERT *eats the bun.* MAY, *glued to the telly, reaches over and feels for the bun. It isn't there. Puzzled, she goes to the kitchen for another bun.*

Hm.

She goes out. GROSS *drinks her tea. She returns with another bun. Places it on the arm of the sofa.* STANLY *suddenly rises, pushes the cat off his lap.*

Aw.

The cat falls to the floor, dead. STANLY *runs his hand through his hair.*

Huh.

STANLY *grunts, then shambles off to the toilet.*

(*Calling after* STANLY): Goin' toilet are 'e? (*To the* BODY:) 'E ab'm done that since 1962. 'E've bin toilet since 1962, several times, but 'e ab'm woke up, partway through our favourite programme, an' chose to go at this particular time.

She notices the cat.

Hm. Cat's died now. Bloody funny. We've 'ad that cat fourteen year. Gone an' died on us. Musta bin the shock a Stanly wakin' up. Creatures of 'abit, cats. Good bit comin' up now.

She takes her cup and leans forward to watch the telly. She drinks from it but there is no tea. She looks at the BODY.

Hm.

She looks round. The heads duck from the window.

Stanly! You drunk my tea? You see? Who drunk my tea? Stanly? Where be 'e? Damme! Stanly!

STANLY *returns.*

STANLY: 'S'at dead body doin' in the toilet?

MAY: Another one?

STANLY: Sittin' on the bloody seat.

MAY: Someone musta put it there. Is it dead?

STANLY: Course it is. 'Tis caked wi' mud.

MAY: Still there?

STANLY: I aren't gonna shift'n. 'Ad to piddle on the crocuses.

MAY: Aw. (*She looks at her empty cup.*) Anyone out there?

STANLY (*matter of fact*): 'Alf the parish.

MAY: Hell.

STANLY: Gilbert got a wet trouserleg.

MAY: Cat's died.

STANLY: Aw.

He starts to shamble out. MAY *isn't too keen to be left alone. She rises and goes to the door after him. Calls after him.*

MAY: Where you goin'?

STANLY (*off*): Set traps for rats!

MAY: Why!?

STANLY (*off*): Cat's died!

MAY *stands with her back to* GROSS. *He checks the time but being naked he isn't wearing a watch. He looks at the clock and takes the cat up onto his lap.* GRACE *screams loud like a cat.* MAY, *with an intake of breath, turns and sees the cat on the* BODY's *lap. She screams.*

MAY: Oo! Stanly! Stanly!

STANLY (*off*): Now what?

MAY: Come back! Cat id'n dead! 'E juss screamed!

STANLY *comes back. He holds a rat trap, set. He goes to the front of the sofa. Puts the trap on the floor near* GROSS's *foot, and takes the cat off* GROSS's *knee. Shakes it, throws it back on the floor.*

STANLY: That cat's dead.

MAY: 'Ow d'e git on the body's knee?

STANLY: Rigor mortis.

MAY: Summin' bloody fishey goin on 'ere Stanly.

STANLY: Is there?

MAY: Two dead bodies, dead cat screamin', missin' bun, drunk tea...

STANLY *indicates bun on sofa arm.*

STANLY: Bun's there.

MAY: Thass another bun.

STANLY: Where's the other bun?

MAY: Tis missin'!

STANLY *starts to shamble towards the kitchen.*

Where be goin'?

STANLY: Git a bun.

MAY: There id'n another bun. This 'ere's the last one!

STANLY *makes for the kitchen.*

Stay 'ere!

STANLY (*off*): Gonna make some tea!

MAY: Wait for me!

She runs off after him. GROSS stands and puts his foot in the rat trap. It snaps shut on his toe. He hops and screams in agony, all over the room, he manages to contain himself. GILBERT leaps through the window, steals the other bun and jumps out again, pocketing it as he goes. GROSS sits back on the sofa but doesn't have time to remove the trap from his foot because MAY and STANLY peer through the door. GILBERT and ALICE peer in through the window. MAY and STANLY creep into the room and peer round.

What was it Stanly? What was that noise?

STANLY: East wind.

He goes to the sofa to take the bun, which isn't there.

Aw.

He looks round for it but notices the TV.

Aw. Favourite programme.

He takes the cat and places it on his lap. Falls promptly back to sleep and starts to snore. MAY returns tentatively to her seat, watches the TV, warily. She notices after a second or two the trap attached to GROSS's toe throbbing. She stands and circles it, trips on STANLY's foot. Screams.

Uh?

MAY: Stanly. The rat trap.

STANLY: What?

MAY: 'Tis sprung shut. 'Cross the body's foot.

STANLY (*half asleep*): Rigor mortis.

MAY: 'E got a throbbin' toe. 'Tis swellin' up blue. Stanly.

STANLY: Go an' make the tea.

MAY: Dead bodies dun't swell up blue Stanly. Throb?

STANLY: Do.

MAY (*to the* BODY): Who are you? You bin sent to visit me? From a divine source? Are you a messenger from God? What tidin's have you brought me? Tell me 'bout Moses, an' the locusts.

The BODY emits a low, keening sound. MAY drops to her knees in supplication. The BODY raises its foot, slowly, and offers it to MAY. She takes it, removes the trap, and kisses the toe. The BODY yelps in agony. MAY springs back and on her feet.

Stanly. Go out. He want to talk to me alone. Go on Stanly.

STANLY *wanders out and round the back, he looks in through the window.*

Speak, oh Prophet.

GROSS (*mumbles clearly*): An' the lord said unto Moses, ye shall eat locusts. An' the bald locust, and all of his kind.

GILBERT, *at the window, pulls a face.*

An' the ferret, an' the lizard, an' the mole, these shall be an abomination unto you . . .

GILBERT (*to* ALICE): Thank Christ for that.

MAY *clutches her bosom and turns her head to heaven.*

MAY: Speak to me Lord, for tonight you have touched me with your divinity, my heart is chastened, my soul pure, an' my body strong, give me strength Lord, an' I will do your biddin'! If you 'ave chosen me to spread your message throughout the land . . .

GROSS, *who can sense his triumph slipping out of his hands, leaps up and yells.*

GROSS: 'COURSE 'E AB'M YOU BLOODY 'OLE BAT!

MAY *screams and faints into an armchair. GROSS turns to the window. He points at* MAY.

See that! See that!

GILBERT *leaps through the window. He is handcuffed to* STANLY, *who is handcuffed to* ALICE. *They naturally follow him in.*

GILBERT: Now thun. Whass goin' on?

GROSS: See that Gilbert?

GILBERT: You'm under arrest.

GROSS: Whass up?

GILBERT: Breakin' an' enterin', causin' Mrs May to faint, killin' a domestic cat, an' impersonatin' a dead body.

GROSS: I'm Archie Gross!

GILBERT: Thass another one.

GROSS: What?

GILBERT: Impersonatin' Archie Gross.

GROSS: I *am* Archie Gross!

GILBERT: You're not Archie Gross. Archie Gross dun't land 'isself in the shit like 'iss. Archie Gross is a schemin', clever man. Archie Gross lead where others follow. Archie Gross is a respected member of the community. Buster. You id'n no Archie Gross. You'm an alien. Where's your passport?

He releases himself from the handcuffs and connects GROSS *to the other two.*

GROSS: Look at my face! Look! Underneath the mud! There's Archie Gross! Damme your sister's married to my son!

GILBERT: C'mon. In the toilet. I got business to conduct.

He leads them out. GROSS *limps.*

GROSS (*as he goes*): Any witch-hazel in the toilet Stanly?

STANLY: No.

GROSS: Got a bad toe.

They are out. MAY *starts to come round.* GILBERT *returns with the* BODY *and the toilet key. He places the* BODY *on the sofa and climbs out through the window.* MAY *wakes up and stands. She walks to the* BODY *and peers into its face.*

MAY: Still 'ere are 'e? I got a damn good idea now whass goin' on and if you think you can get one up on me Archie Gross tis a damn sight 'arder'n you think!

She twists the BODY's *ear. No response. Pinches its arm. No response. Checks its toe. White, bloodless, not swollen. She screams again and yells for* STANLY. *There's a muffled shout from the toilet. She shouts for* STANLY *again and a Pan Am bag appears at the window. At last she is struck dumb.* GILBERT *follows the bag through the window. He dumps it on the settee and shows her its contents.*

Whass this?

GILBERT: Pan Am bag. Under arrest.

MAY: Uh?

GILBERT: Where's your passport?

MAY *produces her passport as if by magic from her apron pocket.*

MAY: 'Ere.

GILBERT, *thrown by the fact that someone's actually got a passport, feels he ought to check it, so he does.*

'Tis all stamped an' up to date.

GILBERT *pockets it.*

GILBERT: Hm.

MAY: Whass the money for? Good works?

GILBERT: The body.

MAY: You wanna buy it?

GILBERT: Thass my orders.

MAY: Hell.

GILBERT: So. You'm under arrest.

MAY: What for?

GILBERT: Er, harbourin' a divine body, thass an offence for a start. You gotta turn over aliens for quarantine.

MAY: That body id'n divine. 'Tis dead.

GILBERT: 'E quoted the scriptures at ya! I 'eard'n.

MAY: That was Archie Gross!

GILBERT: Archie Gross is locked in the toilet Missus, 'long wi' Stanly an' Alice.

MAY: What 'e arrested Stanly for?

GILBERT: Possession of a gas mask.

MAY: What about this money thun?

GILBERT: I'll 'ave that.

He takes the money and handcuffs MAY *to the body.*

Wait 'ere.

He goes out to the toilet. MAY *kneels before the* BODY *and makes absolutely sure it's dead. The* FARMERS *of the parish enter silently through the window and stand in a line behind the settee with their hands behind their backs. They study* MAY *examining the* BODY. GILBERT *returns with the other three.* MAY *looks up.*

MAY: This body is dead y'know Stanly.

STANLY: Course 'tis bloody dead. 'Tis stinkin' the place out! Why the 'ell d'you think I bin wearin' a gas mask for three days!

GILBERT *releases* MAY *from the* BODY *and handcuffs her to* STANLY. *The* FARMERS *speak to the audience. While they speak* GILBERT *goes behind them and handcuffs them all together, and finally to* MRS MAY.

FARMERS:
We, the farmers of this parish,
Have noticed
Nothing much
Amiss.
Little to take our minds
Off the ripening wheat
Has come to pass.
We were warned of chaos,
Warned, we ignored it,
Completely.
United we stood
As here we stand
Before you.
Depleted
But wholesome.
Shorn,
But uncontaminated.
Worn down
But self-contained.
Pious, smug,
Opinionated,
Generally healthy.

They are all handcuffed. GILBERT *hustles everyone out. As he goes he jabs a finger at the* BODY.

GILBERT (*to the* BODY): You stay 'ere.

They go out. The lights close up on the BODY *and the dead cat on the floor. The* BODY *slowly moves. It leans forward. Takes the cat up and places it on its lap, strokes it, looks at the audience and speaks.*

BODY: I'd like to tell y'all a story. But before I begin, we have to go back, to the beginning . . .

The lights fade to blackout.

Part Two

Early morning. A bright summer's day. A dead MARINE *lies centre stage.* WALT *stands guard by the fence. Larks sing. A jet takes off and flies overhead. Larks sing. The dead* MARINE *sits up and tells a story to the audience.*

BODY: When I was alive, towards the end of my life – by the way I'm dead right now, I died, close on five minutes ago – I had a fear of yawning. Got to figuring if I yawned too hard the skin round my lips, when they opened wide, would peel right back over my head and down my neck and turn me inside out. I started to yawn when I was sixteen, back home, when I was bored. I know that healthy guys when they hit sixteen start to do things other than yawn. But believe me where I came from there was little hope of that. And yawning was the next best thing. One day my paw caught me yawning. He said, 'Son, join the marines.' (*Here, as the* BODY *talks,* WALT *starts humming to himself, 'The Star Spangled Banner'.*) I said, 'Paw I'm bored'. He said, 'The marines will sure kick the shit outa that.' So. I enlisted. First thing they do is cut my hair off. Which kinda makes me uneasy cus by now I'd reached neurosis point about this skin peeling business, and I figured the only thing which would stop the skin from shooting right back over the top of my skull when I yawned was the hair. Figured it might like hold it in check long enough for me to yank it all back into place. But on my first day . . . had my head shaved . . . believe me I kept my mouth tight shut. But, by the end of my training at boot camp on Parris Island I was a highly-tuned killing machine, prepared to be sent to any part of the world, get shot up and die protecting the free world from the onslaught of Communism. Paw was right. Sure kicked the shit outa yawning. I was ready to kill. Go over the top. I had a weapon in my hand and my finger itched to squeeze the trigger. Got to figure if it itched much more it'd drop off. I had visions of me, under fire, storming a tree line in a fire fight and comin' up face to face with a big Soviet stormtrooper and there I am weapon in hand ready to blast the bastard to boot hill finger on the trigger and the damn thing's itchin' so much it drops off. We were issued with ointment anyhow to relieve the ... er, but, what happens? I'm sent here. Guarding warheads. Sitting on top of that observation tower, which, thank Christ was made unsafe by the last gale, and walking up and down the fence, guarding warheads against sheep! I started yawning again. Twice, three times a day. Then it hit me. We were trained to kill, and to die. Now I dunno whether any a you good people are dead, but if you are still alive, the one thing that bothers us about dying is what happens after. I only died five minutes ago but it strikes me being dead is much the same as being alive. It's boring. I think I've bin sent to hell. Don't die. I made a mistake. I erred. It's hell all right. So. I'm dead. And in hell.

He lies down again. Dead. The LIEUTENANT *walks on, he joins* WALT *and they marchez sur place around the perimeter.*

WALT: Good day lieutenant.

LIEUTENANT: Oh hi, er, Walt. Hear the larks?

WALT: Sure can sir.

BODY:
This is my lieutenant,
In charge of my platoon.
I never thought we'd meet
Again so soon.
And his promotion hunting
Ass lickin' sergeant.
These are the reasons
I went!

LIEUTENANT: Have we developed a weapon yet Al, that's effective against larks?

WALT: Not to my knowledge sir.

LIEUTENANT: Hm. Goddam larks. Drive me crazy. Grates the nerves, the sound they make. Counted the sheep Walt?

WALT: Sir. All there.

LIEUTENANT: And the warheads?

WALT: Still here sir.

LIEUTENANT: Checked on the people?

WALT: They're going about their business.

LIEUTENANT: Fence OK?

WALT: No holes sir.

LIEUTENANT: What about this observation tower?

WALT: I spoke to Jack Steeple the steeplejack sir he says he happens to have a steeple he could build cheaper than a new tower. This steeple, strengthened, would withstand gales. It has a bell tower and spiral staircase.

LIEUTENANT: Some steeple ...

WALT: So ...

LIEUTENANT: Build it. Who's this?

They come upon the BODY.

WALT: This is Bud sir.

LIEUTENANT: What is he doing? Lying, inert, on the grass?

BODY: I'm dead.

WALT: He's dead sir.

LIEUTENANT: Before chow? How did he die?

BODY: Boredom.

WALT: He was bored sir.

LIEUTENANT: Well let's move on and think about him after chow. I'm hungry.

WALT: Pardon me lieutenant I think its more pressing than that.

LIEUTENANT: How's that Al?

WALT: He died of boredom sir.

LIEUTENANT: Hell.

BODY: It sure is.

WALT: We gotta lotta marines here who think there's more to life than counting sheep, they are all bored. If they hear he has died of boredom, then boredom becomes a bona fide means of death. They'll start dropping like flies. I dunno. I might even die.

BODY: Please Walt, no.

LIEUTENANT: Please Al, no.

WALT: Well sir.

LEIUTENANT: I get your angle Al. Oh here's Walt.

They come upon AL, *who's on guard duty.*

WALT: I'm Walt, this is Al.

LIEUTENANT: Oh. (*To* WALT:) Hi

Walt, I was just saying to Al here . . .

WALT: You were saying it to me . . .

LIEUTENANT: Was I? What was I saying?

AL: These goddam larks drive me crazy.

LIEUTENANT: That's right. (*To* WALT:) You're confusing me Al . . .

WALT: Walt!

AL (*to somebody, off*): Halt!

LIEUTENANT: What's up Walt?

AL (*going off*): Hey shitkicker, what the fuck d'you think y'doing?

KENNETH (*off*): Pickin' mushrooms.

LIEUTENANT: Better lie down Walt you never know . . .

He drops and hides behind the BODY, face to the ground, hands over head. WALT and AL go to the edge of the stage.

BODY: Soon as I die there's action.

AL (*to KENNETH, who is on the other side of the fence*): You're standing thirty metres from a weapons store containing enough plutonium to devastate Moscow and you tell me you're picking mushrooms? Take a look at this Walt. Put your hands on your head.

KENNETH: I own this field.

WALT *ambles up.*

AL: Says he owns this field.

KENNETH: Look, I'm wearin' bedroom slippers.

WALT: So what?

KENNETH: I'm not a spy.

WALT: Who said anything about spies?

KENNETH: I used to own the field you're in, before it was requisitioned.

WALT: Requisitioned . . .

AL: He was requisitioned.

KENNETH: I'm wearin' bedroom slippers.

AL: Take 'em off.

KENNETH: There are thistles!

WALT and AL: Thistles!

They advance on him menacingly and stand, weapons levelled. He remains rigid.

AL: Come on.

KENNETH *shuffles forward.*

WALT: Take off your left slipper. Throw it over there. Now the right. Put your hands on your head and advance to the fence.

KENNETH *advances to the fence but with difficulty as his bare feet keep stepping on thistles.*

WALT: The warheads in that bin are medium range Thistle DX 43's. Where did you obtain this intelligence?

KENNETH: You juss tole me.

AL: This guy knows something.

He lifts the fence.

AL: *Entrez.*

KENNETH *crawls under the fence. They walk to the LIEUTENANT. He raises his head.*

LIEUTENANT: Oh it's Kenneth. Hi Kenneth.

KENNETH: Ullo.

LIEUTENANT (*rising*): Well Kenneth, just a routine investigation, before chow.

They investigate KENNETH as the BODY speaks.

BODY:
It's only Kenneth.
Poor bastard.
I dunno why
They bring him
In here.
Plain as day
He ain't no spy.

WALT: Sir I have a plan. It's a wild, crazy idea which might just work.

LIEUTENANT: What's that Walt?

WALT: Take your clothes off Kenneth.

KENNETH: Uh?

WALT: Do as I say turdbird!

He levels his weapon at KENNETH. KENNETH strips to his underpants as they speak.

Al, strip the body.

AL: Sure thing Sarge.

BODY: Oh, this could be interesting.

LIEUTENANT: What'n hell's going on?

WALT *takes the* LIEUTENANT *downstage.*

WALT: Sir Bud's death must be covered up. We cannot let it be known he died of boredom. In two month's time our battalion is gonna be posted, who knows where. If we can hold on, for two months, then Bud can be lost in the withdrawal. But right now he's gonna be missed. My plan is this: We substitute Bud, with Kenneth. The guys here are so bored they'll never notice the switch. But at least we'll have a Bud.

LIEUTENANT: Walt this plan stinks. Kenneth old Buddy put your clothes back on.

KENNETH *starts to dress.* WALT *draws the* LIEUTENANT *further downstage.*

WALT: Sir, you're ambitious . . .

LIEUTENANT: Am I?

WALT: You hope to make general by the time you're forty-five.

LIEUTENANT: I do?

WALT: You have an imaginative, individual streak in you which makes your command special. You are iconoclastic. In this mass, conglomerate fusion of wills, which is the marines, your will stands out, on elastic.

LIEUTENANT: Oh really?

WALT: It's the measure of a good peace-time command lieutenant that your men are seen to be happy and fulfilled. We are trained to die by the bullet sir, not by boredom.

LIEUTENANT: You have a point there Al. Kenneth take your clothes off . . .

KENNETH *strips.*

WALT: I hope, sir, that when it comes to promotion you won't confuse me with Al.

LIEUTENANT: Oh I'm sure that right after I'm promoted names will come real easy.

He walks back to KENNETH.

Kenneth, er, Walt and me have bin chewing things over. How would you like to join the marines? Spend a coupla months this side of the fence?

KENNETH: I got to grease the combine.

LIEUTENANT: Holy Toledo. Hear that Walt? Any other pressing engagements Kenneth?

KENNETH: Well there's the dance tomorrer night . . .

LIEUTENANT: Oh? Where?

KENNETH: Parish 'all. Me wife drag me off to these does an' we 'ave to prat about all night long. I aren't that keen on it reely.

WALT: Who's playing?

KENNETH: Manny Cockle and the big four combo.

LIEUTENANT: Walt, I think we should take this in don't you?

WALT: I should say so, sir.

LIEUTENANT: Should I wear my uniform?

WALT: Well, lieutenant, there's Mavis Rickeard, who likes a man in uniform, but Alice . . .

LIEUTENANT: Oh, Alice . . .

WALT: I recall, Alice caught your eye last time, at the hunt ball.

LIEUTENANT: And how . . . Alice . . .

WALT: Well she's keen on a tweed jacket.

LIEUTENANT: This is the latest intelligence we have on Alice now Walt . . .

WALT: This is intelligence gleaned from the most reliable source in the field, sir.

LIEUTENANT: Who's that Walt?

WALT: Gilbert the policeman sir.

KENNETH: Hah!

LIEUTENANT: He told you Alice falls for a guy in a tweed jacket?

WALT: No sir. I was listening outside the police station window when she and Gilbert were quarrelling on the subject.

LIEUTENANT: And this is recent intelligence?

WALT: This is tomorrow, sir.

LIEUTENANT: Hell. You mean to tell me that you have gathered intelligence, verifiable information, that hasn't happened yet?

The Body

by Nick Darke

CAST IN ORDER OF APPEARANCE

The Villagers

The Farmers of the parish	Christopher Bowen, William Haden, Brian Parr
Grace Gross	Jenny Agutter
Kenneth Gross, her husband	Clive Wood
Mrs May	Brenda Peters
Alice	Lesley Sharp
Archie Gross, Kenneth's father	Christopher Benjamin
Gilbert the Policeman, Grace's brother	David Shaw-Parker
The body	Tom Mannion
The Rector	Derek Godfrey
Stanley, Mrs May's husband	Jimmy Gardner

The Americans

Walt	Pete Postlethwaite
The Lieutenant	John Bowe
Al	Niall Padden

Musicians

Timothy Hayes Music Director/keyboards
Jonathan Hess saxophone/flute
Peter Chapman bass
Tony McVey drums

Directed by **Nick Hamm**
Designed by **Dermot Hayes**
Music by **Guy Woolfenden**
Lighting by **Michael Calf**
Company voice work by **David Carey**
Voice Coach **Joan Washington**
Stage Manager **Trevor Williamson**
Deputy Stage Manager **Jill Macfarlane**
Assistant Stage Manager **Stephen Dobbin**

There will be one interval of 15 minutes.

Premiere performance of this production: The Pit, 22 April 1983.

An earlier version of *The Body* was performed by the Guildhall School of Music and Drama, directed by Peter Clough, on 19 October 1982.

The Pit is the Royal Shakespeare Company's small theatre in the Barbican Centre. It continues the traditions of its London predecessor, The Warehouse, and of the Company's small Stratford theatre, The Other Place, both of which were converted from rehearsal spaces into intimate auditoria with seating on three or four sides.

We would like to thank the following people for their help on this production:
Callard & Bowser Nuttalls Ltd, for Nuttalls Mintos
J. Sainsbury for foodstuffs.

Wardrobe care by Persil, 'Frend' and Robin Starch
Tights by Elbeo

Production photographs by Alastair Muir.

Play Notes

In the sixth century BC the Greeks embarked on the scientific adventure which landed us on the moon. That surely is an impressive growth curve. But the sixth century BC also saw the birth of Taoism, Confucianism and Buddhism: the twentieth of Stalinism, Hitlerism and Maoism. There is no discernible curve. We can control the motions of satellites orbiting the distant planets but cannot control the situation in Northern Ireland. Prometheus is reaching out for the stars with an empty grin on his face and a totem-symbol in his hand.

The Heel of Achilles **Arthur Koestler**

Imagine the idea that science had developed over the last 200 years at an unnatural rate, obscuring the fact that social advancement, has stood still. We still cling to religious beliefs, still fight ridiculous wars, treat each other and our fellow animals barbarically, still encourage and sustain values and moral codes which are selfish, violent, aggressive, and nationalistic. Suspicion of new social ideas, hatred of an alien race or culture, are still ingrained in us as they were before the steam engine whistled, before telephone bells rung, before microchips buzzed, before nuclear weapons threatened us with extinction.

Nick Darke

Programme notes compiled by Ellen Goodman

Credits

Royal Shakespeare Theatre
Incorporated under Royal Charter
Patron Her Majesty the Queen
President Sir Harold Wilson
Chairman Sir Kenneth Cork
Vice Chairman Dennis L Flower

Royal Shakespeare Company
Joint Artistic Directors
Terry Hands, Trevor Nunn
Direction
Peggy Ashcroft, John Barton, Peter Brook,
Terry Hands, Trevor Nunn
Consultant Director Sir Peter Hall

The Pit
Paul Armstrong *Assistant Electrician*
Sally Barling, Sue Storr *Pit Administrators*
Giles Barnabe *Production Manager*
Stephen Browning *Publicity*
Michael Calf *Chief Electrician*
Judith Cheston *Press*
Keith Clarke *Chief Stage Technician*
Carol Fowler and Frances Reid
 Wardrobe Mistresses
Joyce Nettles *Casting*
Phil Parker *First Stage Technician*

Smoking is not permitted in The Pit
Please do not use tape recorders or cameras

In the event of having to evacuate the building, there are two emergency exits: from The Pit foyer to the ramps on Level 6; and from the right of the auditorium to Silk Street. Please follow the instructions of management and staff.

The Bar in the Cinema foyer serves drinks during the interval. Ice creams will be on sale in The Pit foyer. Toilets (including one for the disabled) are located in the Cinema foyer.

The RSC is

The Barbican Theatre and The Pit are part of the Barbican Centre for Arts and Conferences, built and paid for by The Corporation of the City of London as a gift to the nation.

Pit Licensees: The Corporation of the City of London.

WALT: The purest form of intelligence when you think about it sir. Impossible to deny, because it hasn't happened yet, and yet, confirmable, because international law states that a future event is verifiable up until it has taken place and been denied. In the event of a denial, of course it hasn't happened, in international law, even if it did.

LIEUTENANT: Did it?

WALT: Yes sir.

LIEUTENANT: When?

WALT: Tomorrow sir.

LIEUTENANT: Who's on guard duty tomorrow night Walt?

WALT: Bud sir.

LIEUTENANT: But he's dead.

WALT: Is he sir?

LIEUTENANT: That's his body.

WALT: That's yesterday's intelligence, sir. I see tomorrow's Bud standing here right before you. Full of life and bursting with energy.

LIEUTENANT: It works Walt.

WALT: He isn't keen on dancing sir.

LIEUTENANT: Is that correct?

KENNETH: Me? I aren't that keen no. Could live without it.

LIEUTENANT: He could live without it. He's alive.

WALT: What did I tell you sir?

LIEUTENANT: This is clairvoyance, Walt. So long as it happens. Then you don't mind standing guard duty whilst we go and dance?

KENNETH: I got to grease the bloody combine, mister! International!

AL: 'S a fuckpig to grease . . .

WALT: Have a cigar Kenneth.

KENNETH: Aw. Thanks.

WALT: Beer? American. The best.

KENNETH: Wouldn' say no.

WALT *lights* KENNETH's *cigar and offers him a beer. They wander downstage.* KENNETH *in his socks and underpants.* WALT *speaks urgently to* KENNETH.

WALT: Got a guy here died a boredom Kenneth. The bear is sitting on your back doorstep, just waiting for the chance to walk in. Boredom is a disease, which spreads. Could wipe out a battalion inside a two months. Imagine what havoc the pinkoes could wreak with that kinda propaganda. Bud's death must not leak. I'm offering you a chance to serve your country. And the whole of western democracy. The freedom of Europe and the free world lies in your hands. Sorta freedom that allows you to enter a field a farmer and exit a marine. Come brother. Be Bud.

KENNETH *ruminates. He puffs on his cigar and drinks his beer. He swaggers a bit. As he speaks* AL *hums the tune of 'The Star Spangled Banner', absently, to himself.*

KENNETH: Oft, while traversin' a field, my stride becomes a swagger. My round shoulders square up and these brows knit against a scorching sun. Where a dutch barn stood, a wagon rolls. Where bullocks grazed, buffalo chew. A rabbit scampers, and an injun falls. John Wayne comes to mind as I drawl a command to the cavalry and rooks circle, like vultures, high above the plain . . .

LIEUTENANT: Welcome Bud.

AL: Howdy.

KENNETH: Howdy.

BODY: Nicely put Walt.

WALT (*to* KENNETH): Thanks Bud.

LIEUTENANT (*acidly*): Nicely done, Walt.

AL: Mustard sarge.

WALT: Thanks Al. What to do with the body, sir?

LIEUTENANT: Ah. Well. You know the marines treat their dead comrades with the greatest respect, this is a tradition we're proud to uphold . . .

WALT: We're mighty close to the cliff . . .

BODY: Oh Christ bury me please. Dig a pit right here and cover me over . . .

LIEUTENANT: We could pitch him over the cliff . . .

WALT: Exactly how I read it, sir.

LIEUTENANT: Good. I'm glad I thought of it first. Pitch it over the cliff sergeant. Al help him out there. I'm gonna fix me some chow and dig out a tweed jacket. Kenneth slip into some pants willya an' I'll lock y'in to the routine of things over chow and callisthenics.

WALT and AL remove the BODY and KENNETH picks over BUD's uniform. As the BODY is carried out he waves to the audience.

BODY: Talk to you later.

The LIEUTENANT sits while he waits for KENNETH.

LIEUTENANT: That Walt. He thinks of every goddam thing. For chrissakes Bud who's the fucking lieutenant round here! Uh? I gotta think of something someday! I gotta teach that bastard smartassed sergeant a lesson! I'm iconoclastic Bud. In this mass conglomerate er, confusion of wills my will stands out on elastic. I hope to make general by the time I get to forty- five. I gotta see action to do that. I can't sit on my ass taking shit from a dumb turdbird sergeant who makes out he's some kinda guru! He makes things happen before they happen that's all! That's so simple it's stupid. It's so stupid I could think of something like that. Some day. But Walt has it coming to him. He's gonna get his.

The larks, which have been singing all through this scene, have reached prominence. The LIEUTENANT notices them in the sky. He aims his weapon and fires a burst of automatic fire into the air. KENNETH, now dressed in BUD's uniform, falls to the ground, terrified. A dead lark drops on his head. The LIEUTENANT picks the lark up and checks that it's dead.

Things are gonna happen so fast, Bud, Walt won't know which way to look.

KENNETH: How do I look?

LIEUTENANT: Oh you look smart, Bud. C'mon Buddy boy. Let's eat chow.

They go off.

The police station. GILBERT stands behind the desk. He yawns. WALT enters.

He carries a carton of popcorn and a wad of four hundred dollar bills.

WALT: Good day Gilbert. Hard up?

GILBERT: 'Ungry.

WALT: Here's a carton of popcorn.

He places the popcorn on the desk.

GILBERT: Aw. Ta.

WALT: And here's four hundred dollars that says you wear your uniform to the dance tonight.

GILBERT: Eh?

WALT: None of this tweed jacket crap.

GILBERT: I git four 'undred f'r an arrest.

WALT: We have an exacerbation up at the camp. Could repercuss. With me?

GILBERT: All right.

WALT: Talk to you later.

WALT goes. GILBERT remains onstage but removes the popcorn and dollars from the desk and replaces them with a bucket which has a few cockles in the bottom. During the FARMERS' speech he delves for a cockle and eats it raw. The FARMERS of the parish, dressed immaculately in tweed jackets and grey slacks, invite us to the dance.

FARMERS:
We, the farmers of this parish,
Care to inform you
That tonight a dance
Will take place
In our hall.
It gives our youth
The chance
To let its hair down.
And all the day
We look forward to it.
People come from miles around –
Rumford.
And airbase personnel.
Meticulous
In our attire.
Spruce.
We prepare ourselves, well.

GILBERT is down right, leaning on his desk. GRACE sits down centre, applying make-up. STANLY stands in his undershorts stage left, ironing a voluminous dress. The LIEUTENANT stands up right shaving himself. He too is in his underwear. Near him, up left, AL stands, and on the other side of AL, BUD lies blindfolded, field stripping and reassembling an M16. GRACE wears a print dress. STANLY starts to sing 'Girls Were Made to Love and Kiss'. After a bar or two, the LIEUTENANT sings the same song, independently of STANLY. After a few bars GILBERT starts. It's sung as a round.

Song

Girls were made to love and kiss,
And who am I to interfere with this,
Is it well,
Who can tell,
I'm a man, and kiss them when I can.

When BUD has reassembled the M16 the LIEUTENANT stops singing but GILBERT and STANLY carry on.

LIEUTENANT: How's he doin' Al?

AL: Ninety seconds sir.

LIEUTENANT: Good. Taken him through the small units tactics manual?

AL: Sir. Ambushes are murder – what are they?

LIEUTENANT *starts singing again.*

BUD: Ambushes are murder.

AL: And murder is fun.

BUD: And murder is fun.

AL: Didn't hear you shitkicker.

BUD: Ambushes are murder and murder is fun.

AL (*matter of fact*): Hut two three four I love the marine corps.

BUD: Hut two three four I love the marine corps.

AL: Pray for war.

BUD: Pray for war.

LIEUTENANT: Callisthenics Al?

AL: Sir. Chinese pressups fingertips sacakashit nose only on the deck start up hut two faster fuckbird hut two faster . . .

LIEUTENANT: Liberty call's cancelled till I can look this man in the eye and see a marine DI.

AL: He's hacking it, sir.

LIEUTENANT: When you've finished here you can take him on a ten click hump round the perimeter with a 70lb pack on his back and four 81 mortar shells hanging off his belt.

AL: I'll do that thing lieutenant.

LIEUTENANT (*matter of fact*): United States Marines since 1775 the most invincible fighting force in the history of man gung ho gung ho gung ho, pray for war.

BUD and AL (*with ony slightly raised voices*): The United States Marines since 1775 the most invincible fighting force in the history of man gung ho gung ho gung ho pray for war . . .

LIEUTENANT: Oh Alice. I'm yours tonight.

AL: Saddle up motherfucker.

BUD straps a seventy pound pack onto his back and hitches a belt full of mortar shells round his waist. He and AL turn and are marching, marchez sur place. The LIEUTENANT splashes aftershave on, then smoothes his hair, what there is of it. Then he starts to dress, slowly and meticulously, in grey slacks and tweed jacket. Brushing his clothes before he puts them on with a clothes brush his mother gave him. The whole operation takes him the entire scene to complete. GRACE applies make-up, STANLY is ironing, GILBERT is chewing a cockle, BUD and AL are marching.

GRACE: Kenneth's bin gone a day and a half. I'm gettin' worried now, 'bout the dance. No one seems that bothered that 'e's missin', but I gotta go the dance, else people say, 'Where's Grace an' Kenneth, they 'ad a tiff?'

BUD *staggers.*

AL: Git up there move it out shitkicker . . .

They move off.

LIEUTENANT: I'll walk into that dance tonight and pull Alice not because I'm wearing a tweed jacket. No sir. But because I've bin told by wonderboy Walt that Alice goes for a man in a tweed jacket.

MAY *enters dressed in skirt, apron and corset. She goes to STANLY. ALICE enters the police station. ALICE is dressed in a revealing get up.*

ALICE: Ready thun?
MAY: Where's the bucket?
GILBERT: What for?
STANLY: What for?
ALICE: Dance.
MAY: Me bloomers.
GILBERT: I ab'm 'ad me dinner yet.
STANLY: Id'n in the bucket.
ALICE: What 'e got for dinner?
MAY: I knaw. They'm in the roof. Stoppin' up the leak.
GILBERT: Eggy tart I 'ope.
STANLY: Tid'n rainin'.
ALICE: Make sure you drink a glass a milk after you et it. Dun't wanne burpin' egg up whilst we'm waltzin'.
MAY: So what?
LIEUTENANT: That gives me a psychological edge over Gilbert, who . . .
GILBERT: Dun't burp.
LIEUTENANT: Will be wearin' his uniform.
STANLY: Dun't need the bucket. If tid'n rainin'.
LIEUTENANT: He'll wither at the sight of handsome me in a . . .
ALICE: Put on that nice . . .
LIEUTENANT . . . tweed jacket . . .
ALICE . . . tweed jacket you wore to the 'unt ball.
MAY: Where's the ladder?
LIEUTENANT: . . . and go sniff round Mavis Rickeard,
GILBERT: I dunnaw.
LIEUTENANT: . . . who likes a man . . .
GILBERT: Stick to me uniform . . .
LIEUTENANT: . . . in uniform . . .
GILBERT: . . . tonight, I think.
STANLY: What for?
ALICE: Why?
GILBERT: Stick to me uniform.
LIEUTENANT: All I need is a psychological edge to . . .
MAY: Fetch me bloomers out the roof!
ALICE: Bloody 'ell, why?
STANLY: What 'e want your bloomers for?
GILBERT: Cus I like wearin' me uniform!
LIEUTENANT: . . . stimulate her animal instincts and . . .
MAY: Dance! Go dance in ya toad!
LIEUTENANT: . . . I'm irresistible.
ALICE: I dun't wanna go dance wi' no p'liceman I wanna go dance wi' Gilbert!
LIEUTENANT: Alice is mine.
STANLY: Never wore your bloomers to the 'unt ball.
GILBERT: I am my uniform.
MAY: I've 'ad me picture took Stanly. People's gonna be scrutinisin' me. Checkin', sayin', there's Mother May, 'ad 'er picture in the papers. She got 'er bloomers on?
GRACE: On the other 'and and if I go on me own they a say . . .
ALICE: Right thun I'll go dance wi' Benny.
GRACE: . . . 'there's Grace, where's Kenneth?'
STANLY: Aw.
GRACE: 'They 'ad a tiff?'
GILBERT: Benny's a twit.
GRACE: When we ab'm 'ad a tiff.
STANLY: Ladder's in the sheep dip.
GRACE: 'E've just gone. Missin'.
MAY *goes off.*
ALICE: Not 'alf as big a twit as you are.
GRACE: But they a say we've 'ad a tiff.
GILBERT: You go dance wi' Benny I'll arrest the bugger.
ALICE: You arrest Benny I'll smack y'in the mouth.
GRACE: If I say . . .
GILBERT: Come on thun, smack me in the mouth.
GRACE: . . . 'e've gone, missin', they a say, 'Aw, they've ad a tiff.'

PART TWO   31

ALICE *smacks* GILBERT *hard in the mouth.*

GILBERT: OUCH!

GRACE: 'E've gone. Missin'.

GILBERT *walks with purpose round the desk and confronts* GRACE.

GILBERT: Right. You're under arrest. Where's your passport?

GRACE: But we never 'ad a tiff! 'E've juss gone. Missin'.

ALICE: What you gonna do now Mr Chief Constable?

GILBERT: Lock 'e up.

ALICE: Aww, Mr Powerful, I inna fraid a you an' your uniform you take 'at uniform off an' put your tweed jacket on see if you got the guts ta lock me up.

GRACE: If we 'ad a tiff 'e woulda greased the combine.

STANLY *has finished the ironing. He leaves the dress on the ironing board and starts to dress in a tweed jacket and grey slacks.* GRACE *at the same time removes her print dress and dresses in a dress exactly identical to the one she took off.* GILBERT *undresses at the same time. The* LIEUTENANT *is completing his operation. When* STANLY *is dressed and* GILBERT *undressed,* MAY *enters with her bloomers on.* STANLY *takes the dress from the ironing board and* GILBERT *starts to dress in tweed jacket, grey slacks.* GRACE, GILBERT, MAY, LIEUTENANT *all finish dressing at the same time.*

STANLY: There now!

GILBERT: Now what?

GRACE: Wish we'd 'ad a tiff.

MAY: Come along Stanly.

LIEUTENANT (*pleased with his appearance*): Right on your dying ass.

ALICE: DANCE!

LIEUTENANT: Start swooning Alice.

GRACE: If we'd 'ad a tiff . . .

STANLY *takes* MAY's *arm and they start to go out.* STANLY *notices something and looks up.* GILBERT, *reluctant to go, transfers food from his uniform to his tweed jacket and slacks. Chocolate, fairy cakes, cheese sandwiches, cockles, all make the journey from pocket to pocket as* ALICE *stands on and looks.*

STANLY: Hell.

MAY: Now what?

GRACE: . . . they could say what they like.

GILBERT: Got 'ave me dinner first.

STANLY: Started rainin'.

GRACE: And they'd be right!

GRACE *goes off.*

LIEUTENANT: Ready for you now Alice.

ALICE: 'Urry up!

STANLY: Where's the bucket?

MAY: Gilbert got it.

ALICE (*drumming her fingers on the desk, notices the bucket*): 'Oose bucket?

GILBERT: Mrs May's.

STANLY (*a rare moment of power*): Go git the bucket, or take they bloomers off.

MAY *crosses to the station desk.*

MAY: This my bucket?

GILBERT: Yeah.

She takes the bucket. As she goes out she notices GILBERT's *tweed jacket and turns back.*

MAY (*with a glint in her eye*): Smart Gilbert.

GILBERT (*doggy*): 'Kyou.

They all go off.

The dance. The parish hall. The FARMERS *of the parish announce the band.*

FARMERS: Ladies and Gentlemen, fresh from his successful season down the Falmouth Dock an' Rail Rock an' Roll Club, Manny Cockle and the Big Four Combo!

MANNY COCKLE AND THE BIG FOUR COMBO *are wheeled on. He is an extraordinarily greasy prig of a classic macho mould, the* BIG FOUR COMBO *are all very short. He sings 'Once I Had a Secret Cockle'. He croons it in a syrupy, sly, smiley way, calculated to make sensible women cringe and men jealous.* MRS MAY *dances with* STANLY, ARCHIE GROSS *dances with* GRACE. *Whenever* MAY *and* GROSS *glide close they smile and scowl respectively at each other.* ALICE *sits with her legs crossed, on the opposite side of the floor to* MAVIS RICKEARD, *who sits with her legs crossed. She is very tarty and all the men sneak glances at her. The* FARMERS *of the parish all dance with themselves.* BENNY *stands somewhere near* MAVIS *and stares at her. The* LIEUTENANT *enters with* WALT. *The* LIEUTENANT *wears a tweed jacket, collar and tie, grey slacks.* WALT *is in uniform, His eyes find* MAVIS RICKEARD *who looks him up and down, uncrosses her legs and crosses them back the other way. The* LIEUTENANT *cups his hands and shouts in* WALT*'s ear.*

LIEUTENANT: Gilbert here yet!

WALT: Can't see him!

The LIEUTENANT *adjusts his tie and smoothes down his hair. He advances on* ALICE, *offers her a dance, she reluctantly accepts and he sweeps her onto the floor.* GILBERT *enters in his tweed jacket. He eats a slice of apple strudel and rubs his jaw where* ALICE *hit him. He sees* WALT *and shouts in his ear. The* LIEUTENANT *doesn't notice him as his face is buried in* ALICE*'s hair.*

GILBERT: Bin a dead body washed up!

WALT *nods and takes a roll of dollar bills from his pocket. He hands them all to* GILBERT. *He doesn't notice* GILBERT*'s tweed jacket as his eyes are glued to* MAVIS. GILBERT *pockets the money, along with the remains of the apple strudel, rubs the crumbs from his fingers and heads towards* ALICE. *He taps the* LIEUTENANT *on the shoulder and elbows him out of the way, dances with* ALICE. *The* LIEUTENANT, *cold-shouldered, registers alarm at* GILBERT*'s attire and heads for* WALT. *He shouts at him.*

LIEUTENANT: What in hell's going on here sergeant!

WALT: Something wrong Lieutenant?

LIEUTENANT: You bet!

The song comes to an end but the LIEUTENANT *doesn't notice. He keeps on shouting. Heads turn.*

THAT FUCKING POLICEMAN'S WEARING A TWEED JACKET!

WALT: Music's stopped sir.

LIEUTENANT: Where in hell do I stand now with this Alice!

WALT: . . . all make mistakes, sir . . .

LIEUTENANT: That all you have to say?!

WALT: There's bin a dead body washed up, sir . . .

LIEUTENANT: THE HELL THERE HAS!

WALT: I think we should discuss it . . .

LIEUTENANT: I say what we discuss round here and what we don't discuss! You're behaviour towards a senior officer, sergeant, is disgusting! I have it in mind to strip these stripes right off your arm! Right here and now! Right in front of these people here! Right where you stand!

He looks at WALT. WALT *looks at everybody else who are all looking at the* LIEUTENANT. *He is humiliated, he throws his hands to his face and buckles at the knee.*

Oh Mother. Oh my god my god my god. Right. Er, (*Recovering.*) right. Er, strike up the band . . .

MANNY COCKLE (*sings*): One two three o'clock four o'clock cockle, five six seven o'clock eight o'clock cockle, I'm gonna rock, around, the cockle tonight . . . etc.

Everybody starts to jive except the LIEUTENANT. WALT *heads for* MAVIS RICKEARD, *so does* GILBERT. BENNY *heads for* ALICE. GILBERT *arrives at* MAVIS *before* WALT *and snatches her just in time.* GRACE *collars* WALT.

GRACE: Care to dance?

They dance. The FARMERS *dance with each other,* MAY *with* STANLY. *The* LIEUTENANT *is caught in the middle of the floor and can't get out. They all jive round him.*

LIEUTENANT: I'll get my own back on you Walt! You haven't heard the last of this! I'll think of goddam something someday! I will! So help me I will!

He rips off his tweed jacket and stamps on it. MANNY COCKLE *chooses this moment to finish the song. Everyone stands and looks at the* LIEUTENANT *storm out. They then cast their eyes to the tweed jacket in the middle of the floor. A moment of stillness and silence. They all raise their eyebrows, then* STANLY *turns to* MANNY COCKLE *and requests a song.*

STANLY: 'Kiss an Angel Good Mornin'?'

WALT: 'I've Got Everything I need To Drive Me Crazy.'

GILBERT: 'My Way.'

GROSS: 'Jezebel'!

FARMERS: 'Where Have All the Flowers Gone.'

MAY: 'I Believe In Every Droppa Rain'!

To everyone's annoyance, MANNY COCKLE *strikes up 'I Believe'. They all shuffle about with their respective partners, unenthusiastically.* GRACE *leads* WALT *downstage.*

WALT: Do I know you?

GRACE: I'm Kenneth's wife.

WALT: Oh? Who's Kenneth?

GRACE: No. Where's Kenneth?

WALT: How's that?

GRACE: 'E left 'ome yesterday an' 'e ab'm come back.

WALT: That's serious. What make of combine would that be?

GRACE: International.

WALT: Wow. The grease nipples on an International . . .

GRACE: Don't change the subject.

WALT: I'm afraid I don't know the whereabouts of your son.

GRACE: Husband. I'll find 'im.

WALT *leads her to a corner. He sneaks a glance at the dance floor.* GILBERT *is dancing with* BENNY, MAY *with* GROSS, STANLY *with* MAVIS, ALICE *and the* FARMERS *sit with their legs crossed.*

WALT: Let me say this lady. Kenneth is missing. I can't tell you where he is. You have an International needs greasing. We have an international situation to keep under control . . .

GRACE: A man can't disappear without his wife askin' where 'e's to mister. I'll churn the place up till I find 'im . . .

WALT: Whose side are you on lady?

GRACE: I aren't at all sure. All I'm sayin' is, the greasin' bain't what matters most . . .

WALT: Lady we live in times when a simple squirt of grease from a gun, in anyone's hand could shift the delicate balance of things over the edge into the abyss and end in war, yes war. I'm a military man, an old timer, and believe me I've witnessed conflicts occasioned by less significant actions than that. Continue your search by all means, the people of this parish are less concerned about Kenneth than their combine, I know that, but all I can say is one day Kenneth will return. Go home and forget about him. I can't say more than that.

He goes, leaving GRACE *centre stage. Everyone is back dancing with their partners again as* MANNY COCKLE *cranks to a close. They all disperse, leaving* GRACE *standing alone. A few stray notes of music accompany her, as she says nothing, just thinks for a while. She walks up and down, now and again looking as if she might have something to say, but thinks better of it. In the end she faces the audience.*

GRACE: Hm.

She goes off.

The Briefing Room. A large map of the area stands on the wall side by side with a map of the British Isles. The LIEUTENANT *stands with a pointer in front of the maps, facing* BUD, AL, *and* WALT, *who all sit. The* LIEUTENANT *is excited,* WALT *disconsolate. There is a telephone somewhere, and a loudspeaker tannoy.*

LIEUTENANT: It seems the body was washed up here. (*He indicates on the map.*) Beneath the iron bridge. Now luckily the body was covered with mud. But we know that he's male, and white.

This means he could come from anywhere in the Northern hemisphere. My theory is this. He's a Russian.

WALT: Lieutenant . . .

LIEUTENANT: Not one word sergeant. This is my baby. Let's look at the overall picture. We are here. Right on the tip of Great Britain . . .

He indicates Cornwall on the map.

Now Britain is shaped like a funnel.

He produces a funnel from somewhere, like magic. He holds it up to the map to illustrate his point. The narrow end is Cornwall.

If you were planning an insurgency operation. A propaganda mission aimed at the psychological overthrow of a nation, where would you land your agents? I wouldn't pour them in, at the top of the funnel. You'd need an army, no, I would *invert* my funnel, and have them enter, the nozzle. (*He points to the tip of the nozzle.*) Gentlemen we have here a nozzle situation, and goddam it, we are the nozzle.

WALT: Lieutenant this body . . .

LIEUTENANT: What is it Smartass?

WALT: Isn't it Bud?

LIEUTENANT: Bud is here.

WALT: No the real Bud. Our Buddy, who we threw over the cliff . . .

LIEUTENANT: Now I didn't hear you say that . . .

WALT: Lieutenant we all know about it here. It's our secret.

LIEUTENANT: That's how it's gotta stay.

WALT: But it's no use trying.

LIEUTENANT: Let me try something now Walt. Bud.

BUD: Sir?

LIEUTENANT: Stand up Bud.

BUD *stands.*

What's your name Bud?

BUD: Bud.

LIEUTENANT (*to* WALT): That's Bud.

WALT: OK. Now the guy, the villager, who's gone missing . . .

LIEUTENANT: Yup . . .

WALT: Kenneth . . .

LIEUTENANT: There must be a cell of at least five agents here already. Maybe more. They've taken Kenneth, he was a perfect shot to start on, round shouldered to denote passivity, impressionable, vague, our file on Kenneth puts him out to be an ideal specimen for brain-washing activities. He'll return in a day or two a perfect pinko who will grease the combine, convert his wife, and thus start the ball rolling . . .

WALT: But isn't he this guy here? Sitting next to me?

LIEUTENANT: Who Bud? Stand up Bud.

BUD *stands*

LIEUTENANT: What's your name Bud?

BUD: Bud.

LIEUTENANT (*to* WALT): That's Bud.

WALT (*exasperated*): But, he's just saying that. He's, he's saying it . . .

LIEUTENANT: Stand up Walt.

WALT *stands.*

What's your name Walt?

WALT: Walt!

LIEUTENANT: You just said it.

WALT: But I *am* Walt. I'm not Kenneth posing as Walt. This is Kenneth, posing as Bud, I'm not dead, washed up, I'm Walt.

LIEUTENANT: Seems to me you're displaying an uncharacteristic lack of imagination this day sergeant.

WALT: I . . .

LIEUTENANT: Could it be you bin pooped? By a man in a TWEED JACKET!?

WALT: Ohh this is bizarre . . .

LIEUTENANT: I dunno whether you know this Walt, but the bear is sittin' on our back doorstep, just waitin' for the chance to walk in . . .

WALT: I told y'all this two days ago . . .

LIEUTENANT: Did you Walt? Ever occur to you that I mighta known about it, BEFORE IT HAPPENED?!

WALT (*the light dawns*): I see. You go right

ahead lieutenant.

LIEUTENANT: What we have here is a pinko takeover of Great Britain. Not by force, but a brilliant, subtle, and blindingly simple, insidious psycho subliminal saturation operation, wrought by experts so devious as to seem, at first sight, to be invincible.

WALT (*to* AL): How can a dead body be invincible.

LIEUTENANT: Wrap it sergeant.

WALT: I'd like to register my opinion of this scenario as bullshit.

The telephone rings. The LIEUTENANT *picks it up.*

LIEUTENANT: Yuh? Yuh. Uh huh. Yeah? *Daily Telegraph*. Court and social . . . wow. (*He takes his hat off.*) Uhh, yuh. WHAT!? MY GOD! Arrest him Gilbert, bring him up here, and fast!

He slams the phone down, glowers at WALT.

Bullshit huh? There's a Chinaman out there! Wandering around! Plain as day! Making out he's the fucking RECTOR!

WALT: Could be a simple explanation.

LIEUTENANT: So the Chinese are in on this. I suspected they would be. They are after all the experts when it comes to subliminal auto-suggestion. What I hadn't bargained for was when. We must act fast . . .

WALT: You're way ahead a me lieutenant.

LIEUTENANT: Then catch up. There's no time to take this higher. We must act on my own initiative.

On another part of the stage GILBERT *and the* RECTOR *walk, handcuffed together, marchez sur place.*

RECTOR: Where be us goin'?

GILBERT: Up the camp.

RECTOR: Ah.

GILBERT: Yuh.

RECTOR: Huh.

GILBERT: If I was a Chinaman I a make damn sure I 'ad a passport with me when I set forth in the parish.

RECTOR: I got a passport someplace, up the vestry.

GILBERT: Thass easy to say buster.

RECTOR: Twas only a li'l joke, this Chinese scat . . .

GILBERT: I'm a p'liceman. My jokes come in uniform. Blue one for a copper. Dog collar for a rector. Off duty tweed jackets is worn. Thass ow it was an' always shall be. (*He rubs his jaw where* ALICE *hit him.*) Bloody Alice.

RECTOR: What?

GILBERT: Smacked me in the gob.

They walk off, towards the camp.

We return to the Briefing Room.

LIEUTENANT: Counter insurgency tactics. We round up anyone, I mean anyone, who has been acting strange, who might have been subjected to severe psychological disarray perpetrated by a red agent. Now, how to go about this. Let's have it from the floor . . . Al.

AL: Lieutenant could I go play Space Invaders?

LIEUTENANT: What's up shithead?

AL: I just ah, I'll do anything you say, my head ain't together this day . . . What wi' no liberty call'n all.

LIEUTENANT: OK you do anything I say, I say you suggest to me a counter insurgency tactical concept.

AL: I think you should round up the whole village, get 'em in here, ask 'em if they're commies, if they say no they're lying so shoot 'em.

They all think about this.

LIEUTENANT: That's good.

AL: Can I go play Space Invaders now?

LIEUTENANT: Let's hear counters to that tactical concept put forward by Al.

WALT: It stinks.

LIEUTENANT: Ah, Sergeant Strategist, has woken up.

WALT: It's a good tactical concept, it's what we're trained to do for chrissakes, but I can see the parallels with Vietnam here. We went in to advise the ARVIN but it didn't work cus we didn' teach 'em right. We blundered and used aggressive patrolling techniques which were not tailored to the geography or the social fabric of the country. I mean do we know what these people eat?

LIEUTENANT: Egg pie, cheese sandwich, fairy cakes, cockles.

WALT: Exactly. I think we should maintain a low profile, train a small guerrilla mission, taking into account their indigenous capabilities, and that way we come up on these bastards from behind.

BUD: Er . . .

LIEUTENANT: What is it Bud?

BUD: Oo's what? You dunno oo's a pinko an 'oo id'n.

AL: Ask 'em! If they say no they're lyin', so shoot 'em.

WALT: Al I think you can go play Space Invaders now . . . here's a dime . . .

LIEUTENANT: No let 'im stay. He's warming to this . . .

WALT: Could Gilbert be the hub of our guerrilla mission? We pay him well so he must be reliable . . .

BUD: Hah!

WALT: Whaddayado with all these Joes once ya got 'em huh?

AL: Shoot 'em!

BUD: Tis brainwashin' we'm talkin' about innit? All the people a bin brainwashed into bein' Joes, we gotta brainwash 'em back again.

AL: Listen turdbird, you're the guy who said he can't tell who from what. You get a guy in here you think is a commie who isn't, you brain-wash him back again to what you think he isn't and he ends up what you don't want him to be and he goes back and starts over brain-washing people who are what you want 'em to be into being something, you have to bring 'em back in here to brain-wash 'em outa being . . .

BUD: Ow dunnus just wait till they'm all brain-washed, then brain-wash 'em all back again . . .

AL: Just shoot 'em for chrissake . . . Go-od.

LIEUTENANT: I think. I can't be positive but I think, Al has a point.

WALT: Getting lost lieutenant? The ultimate decision is yours . . .

LIEUTENANT: Well Walt, in the past you've never been slow to advise me . . .

WALT: It strikes me we have two options. Shoot 'em, or train up Gilbert in counter insurgency by stealth and reverse psychoanalytical subjection.

BUD: Gilbert?

WALT: Yah.

BUD: Shoot 'em.

WALT: He's capable of it, he draws a big salary . . .

LIEUTENANT: In that case, we'll leave it to Gilbert . . .

GILBERT *and the* RECTOR *arrive at the gate.*

RECTOR: How do we get in?

GILBERT: Ring the bell . . .

GILBERT *rings the bell. A bell rings in the Briefing Room.*

LIEUTENANT: Ah, that'll be Gilbert now.

WALT: I'll go get him . . .

WALT *goes out.*

AL: Can I go play Space Invaders now?

LIEUTENANT: Al, let me say something to you. At the end of all this we're gonna be heroes. Now my ambition is to make general by the time I'm forty-five. I'm iconoclastic. In this massed, conglomerate, balloosion of wills, my will bobs out on elastic. And in the end, the reward isn't mine, it's ours. Cus I can't do it on my own. And we will (*Somewhere round here,* BUD *starts humming to himself the tune of 'The Star Spangled Banner'.*) win Al, cus we are God's chosen people. Are you with me Al? No, don't answer, (*Close to tears.*) it was a rhetorical question, because I know, that deep down, you are with me, Al, and I know that Bud here is with me, and dear old Walt is with me. Because we are the chosen. So when next you think of Space Invaders Al, think instead of freedom, of God, his will, and put it out of your mind. I love you Al, I love Bud, and in the end I love dear ole Walt. I want you with me. You're coming along too.

AL: You got me Lieutenant.

LIEUTENANT: That's just fine soldier.

WALT *arrives at the door. He greets* GILBERT.

WALT: Hi Gilbert. This the Chinaman?

GILBERT: Yeah.

WALT: Take the handcuffs off.

GILBERT: All right.

He releases the RECTOR. *The* RECTOR *rubs his wrist.* GILBERT *rubs his jaw.*

WALT: What the fuck you wear a tweed jacket to the dance for last night?

GILBERT: Alice smacked me in the gob . . .

WALT: Put me in the shit you know that?

GILBERT: Sorry.

WALT (*taking a wad of notes from his pocket*): I'm gonna dock you ten dollars . . .

He hands GILBERT *the money bar one note.* GILBERT *places it in his back pocket.*

C'mon in.

He leads them in. As they go, GILBERT *takes from his top tunic pocket, from behind his two-way radio, a gingerbread man. He bites its head off.* WALT *enters the Briefing Room.* GILBERT *and the* RECTOR *follow.*

LIEUTENANT: What's your name?

RECTOR: Rector.

LIEUTENANT: Rector what?

RECTOR: People just call me Rector.

LIEUTENANT: People call me lieutenant, but I have another name, which, for example, my wife calls me.

RECTOR: I aren't married.

LIEUTENANT: Are you a Communist, Rector?

RECTOR: No, I'm a Rector.

LIEUTENANT: A Communist Rector.

RECTOR: Church of England Rector.

LIEUTENANT: Well Rector. Gilbert here tells me you're a Chinaman.

WALT: Unmarried sir, no dependents.

LIEUTENANT: You see you could easily be a Chinaman.

RECTOR: I'm a Rector! I'm too tall to be a Chinaman!

WALT: Up in the North they grow to seven foot tall.

LIEUTENANT: Stand up.

RECTOR: I am!

WALT: If he was a Rector he'd be kneeling sir.

BUD: Praying to get outa here.

LIEUTENANT: So he's an atheist Chinaman posing as a Church of England Rector.

The RECTOR *kneels and turns his face to heaven.*

RECTOR: Please God get me outa here.

WALT: You see he's very short.

RECTOR: I'm kneelin' down!

LIEUTENANT: It's impossible to tell with that rigout on . . .

AL: Shoot him.

RECTOR *stands, holds up his hands.*

RECTOR: No!

AL: Aggressive tactics when threatened. Trained in self-defence! If he was a real Rector in the face of death he'd be counting his beads!

LIEUTENANT: We got him!

AL: Now shoot him!

WALT: Aw go play Space Invaders!

LIEUTENANT: Walt, let me say something to you. At the end of all this we're gonna be heroes. Now my ambition is to make general by the time I'm forty-five . . . In this mass, conglomerate gas station of wills . . .

GILBERT: 'E was speakin' Chinese on the parish 'all steps . . .

LIEUTENANT: Jesus Christ!

AL: The parish hall steps!

LIEUTENANT: Who was there?

GILBERT: Pretty well the whole parish.

LIEUTENANT: Were they listening? Did they understand?

GILBERT: There was a lot listenin' to what 'e 'ad to say. Most I'd say.

LIEUTENANT: How long does it take to learn Chinese Walt?

WALT (*resigned*): Five years sir.

LIEUTENANT: My God they've all bin brain-washed!

WALT: Looks like it sir.

LIEUTENANT: Gilbert. Go round 'em all up. Rector you stay here. Al, go draw some ammunition and patrol the bunkers. They could be planning a takeover of the weapons store.

AL: Sir.

He starts out.

LIEUTENANT: Al!

AL: Sir?

LIEUTENANT: Shoot on sight Al.

AL: Thank *you* lieutenant!

He runs out.

LIEUTENANT: Now then Rector, for such now I believe you to be. We have some brain-washing to be done.

He leads the RECTOR *out by the ear.* BUD *follows.*

GILBERT *and* WALT *are left behind.* WALT *is very disturbed.*

WALT: You and your fucking tweed jacket!

GILBERT: I . . .

WALT: That guy's psychotic, you know that? Means he suffers from abnormal emotional instability. Takes a tweed jacket to trigger off a bastard like that.

GILBERT: Sor-ry.

WALT: Some careers in public life Gilbert that's a smart quality to have. Gets you noticed. Wins votes. But in this scenario its dynamite! Now where'n hell's that body?

GILBERT: Mrs May's.

WALT: Get it.

GILBERT: Now?

WALT: We need evidence. It's a fucking dangerous ballgame Gilbert.

GILBERT: I might 'ave to buy it back.

WALT *takes a Pan Am bag bulging with dollar bills from under the table.*

WALT: Here's a Pan Am bag fulla dollar bills.

GILBERT's *eyes stand out. He grabs the bag, takes it to the table, opens it and starts counting the money.*

GILBERT: My Christ almighty!

WALT *bites his thumbnail and thinks.*

WALT: I gotta brute this mess back into shape. Wire it down. I can't take it higher yet, Joint Chiefs'd laugh in my face . . .

GILBERT: 'Think I swapped the bugger for a bucket of cockles!

WALT: A lieutenant is a lieutenant until he's *proved* to be a psychotic. That's in the small units tactics manual. I must have a case. But proof. What is proof? When any action in this mad world is explicable. Untraceable back to its source. When you're working against a man who might do anything, and find a reason for doing that thing, and twist it to his advantage. Sanity is insanity blessed with authority. Evidence of insanity in that scenario is proof itself of – sanity. The chemistry alters and warps the mind and the minds of those around you till it is I who is insane and the mad one, the psychopath, sane.

GILBERT: Only get four 'undred for a live one . . .

WALT: Where to end it? If innocent people die it doesn't matter. I must walk when he walks. Run when he runs and jump . . . before he jumps. Gilbert.

GILBERT: Yes skip.

WALT: Do as the lieutenant says. Arrest everybody. Buy the body back, then hide it. I'll send Al down to pick it up when we need it. If we live to tell the tale Gilbert there'll be a military hearing. If we don't, we'll be dead. With me?

GILBERT: Yup. Pronto.

WALT: Talk to you later.

GILBERT *starts out with the bag.*

WALT: Gilbert . . .

GILBERT: Yes skip?

WALT: Divulge none a this.

GILBERT *salutes and runs off.* WALT *goes in the opposite direction.*

Music, with a Chinese flavour.
The RECTOR *sits, cross-legged centre stage. He smokes his pipe. His hands are crossed inside the voluminous sleeves of his Chinese cassock. The* LIEUTENANT *paces up and down behind him. We get the sense that the* RECTOR *is serene and things aren't quite going the* LIEUTENANT*'s way. After a while the music stops and the* LIEUTENANT *speaks.*

LIEUTENANT: You mean you're willing to be brainwashed?

The RECTOR *removes his pipe from his mouth, replaces his hand up his sleeve. The pipe goes too.*

RECTOR: I'm beggin' to be brainwashed.

LIEUTENANT: Why Rector? Why?

RECTOR: Because I'm a tired man. I'm tired of sayin' things to those who hear an' dun't listen. I ask 'em when do your children first learn to kill? When you scat the bugger 'cross the ear to stop'n bawlin? When you tell'n scat the bugger back who juss scat you? I say what do it matter who got what? You take 'at I give 'e a scat. That id'n the way to go on. Got to the point now where we got iron out all that scat . . .

LIEUTENANT (*to himself*): Sheeit. That's enigmatic.

RECTOR: I'm tired of seein' things in a helpless light. I'm juss tired a life. Perhaps if you brainwash me into bein' something I'm not, might give me fresh 'ope. Might make me see things in a different way.

LIEUTENANT: The process of brainwashing is threefold Rector. First, you break the victim down. Upset his mental equilibrium, question his validity as a Chinaman. Second, you convince him of the hopelessness of being a Chinaman. You then build him up again, having infused in him the advantages of being a rector. Seems to me you're at a stage three already. But how in hell can I be sure?

RECTOR: How can you be sure of anything?

LIEUTENANT: Sheeit. That's Confucian.

RECTOR: How can you be sure I'm a Chinaman. If you brainwash me I might start out a Rector. And end up a Chinaman.

LIEUTENANT: I see now what Al was getting at.

RECTOR: And if I arrive at bein' a Chinaman, how will you tell?

LIEUTENANT: That's sure a simple one to answer!

RECTOR: Well?

LIEUTENANT: You *are* a Chinaman for chrissakes!

RECTOR: Then brainwash me.

LIEUTENANT: Dammit rector I sure as hell will!

Music. The path to the camp. GILBERT *strides marchez sur place. Behind him in a line, handcuffed together, are* MAY, STANLY, GROSS, ALICE *and three* FARMERS *of the parish.* GROSS *limps.*

GROSS: Ease the pace Gilbert. Me toe's throbbin.

ALICE: Where be us goin'?

GILBERT: Camp.

ALICE: 'For?

GILBERT: Aren't divulgin'.

ALICE: *Musta* done *summin* wrong.

GROSS: Where's Grace?

ALICE: She scat when she 'eard the 'andcuffs clickin'.

MAY: 'Tis the cat dyin' what baffled me. Cats dun't die sudden. Cats start dyin' the day they'm born. Dun't juss drop dead like 'at. They d'go all mangy and lose their whiskers. They go off their food an' 'uddle. Bloody baffled me that cat.

FARMERS: We, the farmers of this parish . . .

ALICE: Belt up.

GILBERT *takes a bun from his pocket and starts eating it.*

GROSS: Bloody toe's killin' me!

ALICE: Tch!

STANLY: Gilbert!

GILBERT: What?

STANLY: Where d'y git that BUN!

They all march off, to reveal the BODY *sitting in his armchair, with the cat on his lap. He sings a song.*

BODY (*sings*):
I'm the only one left,
It seems.
The rest are arrested
And gone.
And that is, perhaps,
As it should be,
When all is said and done.
We answer only
To the sun.
Who stands in heaven,
Hot and white.
Above God,
In my estimation.
On that day that sun
Is brought down to earth
To burn a hole
In our destination –
Will we,
On that day only,
Think again?

His song comes to an end. He stays in his armchair. He views the next scene from the armchair. From here to the end of the play he is never off, always insinuating himself into the action, being part but unseen. He keeps the cat with him.

The fence. AL *patrols.* GRACE *approaches.*

GRACE: Excuse me . . .

AL: Who the fuck's that? Don't come any closer . . .

GRACE: My name's Grace. Grace Gross. I spoke to you at the dance, remember?

AL: What?

GRACE: I was enquiring after my husband Kenneth . . .

AL: He the guy went missin'?

GRACE: Thass right.

AL: Never spoke to me about it. I never was at the dance. Had my damned liberty cancelled.

GRACE: I didn't recognise you. See you clearly in the moonlight. I've come to say . . .

AL: Don't come any closer.

GRACE *stops as* AL *levels his weapon at her.*

GRACE: I was only gonna say, the man said, at the dance . . .

AL: Who?

GRACE: The man at the dance. A sergeant I think . . .

AL: Woulda bin Walt.

GRACE: Thass right.

AL: What he say?

GRACE: Well I was worried at Kenneth's disappearance, he hadn't greased the combine you see, we have an International . . .

AL: Takes some greasin' . . .

GRACE: An' I was concerned about his well-bein' too, though I wasn't so certain of that I was frightened of bein' alone, that came into it, but Walt said to me how selfish it was to think of myself all the time and how it could spark off an international situation if I carried on lookin' for 'im . . .

AL: How's that?

GRACE: If I carried on lookin' for 'im . . .

AL: You armed?

GRACE: What! No!

AL: Put your hands up.

She does so.

Now advance here.

She advances. He frisks her.

Now say.

GRACE *still has her hands up. She is very frightened.*

GRACE: He was sayin' how greasin' a combine could lead to war if I aren't careful and if I dun't discontinue my search an' I said I aren't fussed about that 'tis my duty to my husband to do all I can to find him . . .

AL: You gotta be damn careful what you're sayin' babe . . .

GRACE: All I'm sayin' is I thought about it and after askin' round an' gettin' nowhere I went an' tole 'is father Archie about it . . .

AL: What?

GRACE: About greasin' the combine . . .

AL: What about it?

GRACE: The International, if 'e could 'elp me, an' now 'e's gone off too . . .

AL: Where?

GRACE: Search me I dunno . . .

AL: Don't you think that's a little dangerous?

GRACE: How do you mean?

AL: Comin' up here and tellin' me all this?

GRACE: I told you, I told you, I've left it be now, all I need is help, from somebody, cus my bosom get in the way, someone with thin arms, Walt or you perhaps, greasin' the combine thass all . . .

AL: I thought you were supposed to be subtle you reds. My God I'm a marine d'you know what that means? Means in the name a God I'm trained to kill! You ask me, you walk up to me plain as day and ask me to come and grease your goddam combine! You said yourself that greasing combines leads to war and that is what you're after is it not?

GRACE: I never said that, Walt said it . . .

AL: If Walt said that, that's good enough for me!

He shoots her with a long burst, then after pumping another dozen rounds into her he lifts her body off the ground and swinging it onto his shoulder, carries it off.

The brig. The RECTOR *sits, as before, cross-legged centre stage, his hands in his sleeves. He is Buddha-like, in a trance. The* LIEUTENANT *leans on the wall, in shirt-sleeves, sweating. He's exhausted after the brain-washing.* BUD, WALT, GILBERT *enter with the* PARISH, *all handcuffed.*

GILBERT: I arrested every bugger I could lay 'ands on. One's missin'.

LIEUTENANT: Who's that?

GILBERT: Grace Gross.

MAY: Just 'appen to be 'is sister.

GILBERT: She runned off.

ALICE: 'Fraid a what 'is mother might say.

MAY: Too fond of 'is stomach.

STANLY: Whass goin' on 'ere?

FARMERS: The farmers of this parish . . .

LIEUTENANT: SILENCE! Seven. That'll do to start with. Time check Bud?

BUD *looks at his watch.* WALT *hands* GILBERT *a massive wad of dollar bills.* GILBERT *pockets them.*

BUD: 22.08.

LIEUTENANT: Good. Lock 'em in here with the rector. Cool 'em off then we'll go into action after chow.

The LIEUTENANT, BUD, WALT *and* GILBERT *go off. The* PARISH *huddles round the* RECTOR. *Music. The* BODY *sings a song. It is a fast rock number with a slow intro.*
Slow intro.

BODY (*sings*):
Now that I am dead,
And my short life is through,
I feel like a new born child,
Whose instincts are but two,
To sleep and suck his mother's breast,
I have no other yearning,
To sleep and suck his mother's breast.
All, the rest,
is learning . . .

Fast verse.

My skin of protection
Was more than complexion
And something to wash in the morning.
It covered my shame
And my greed and my lies
It covered my pride
When I unzipped my flies
It covered my hatred and fawning.
But now that I'm dead
My skin it has fled

PART TWO 41

I'm free of my hang-ups
I'm free of my dreads,
And I'm free of my fear –
Of yawning . . .

Yawn chorus.
The MUSICIANS *play the chorus and the* BODY *yawns an enormous yawn through it. Then he speaks to the* PARISH.

That was the chorus . . . if you feel you can join in, without losing your skin . . . your welcome . . .

He sings the verse once more and then yawns through the chorus. They ALL *yawn with him, except the* RECTOR, *who's in a trance, and* STANLY, *who wears a gasmask. At the end the* BODY *melts into the background and the* PARISH *is still yawning.* MAY *emerges from her yawn and stands. She paces.*

MAY: 'Ow long they 'ad us in 'ere?

STANLY: Siddown.

MAY: 'Tis a disgrace. If I was on speakin' terms with the mayor I a complain. Rector. Rector!

ALICE: 'E's asleep.

MAY: Wake up rector.

The BODY *wakes the* RECTOR.

RECTOR: Uuuugghhhh. (*A long groan.*)

MAY: Uh?

GROSS: Huh!

STANLY: Gyat.

FARMERS: Er . . .

MAY: Yaddap!

ALICE: Hah!

MAY (*to* ALICE): What?

RECTOR: Awww.

MAY: Sshh!

ALICE: Tch!

RECTOR (*sings, weakly*): Arise, ye starvelings from your slumbers . . .

MAY: 'E's singin'.

GROSS: 'Ymn. Singin' 'ymn.

RECTOR (*sings*): Arise ye criminals of want . . .

MAY: Hmm.

RECTOR: For reason in revolt now thunders . . .

MAY: Sound like a Charles Wesley.

GROSS: 'Tis definitely Methodist.

RECTOR: . . . and gone is the age of cant.

MAY: Thass early Methodist. Good strong tune.

RECTOR (*sings in Chinese*).

MAY: Damme 'e've reverted back to Chinese.

STANLY: I dun't like it.

MAY: None of us *like* it Stanly.

GROSS: I never sung that when I was a Methodist.

MAY: Yaddap! Never was a Methodist.

GROSS: Neither was 'e.

MAY: 'E'm a rector! They d'cross fertilise!

ALICE: So 'tis a Methodist 'ymn, so what.

MAY: Sing it again Rector. Rector!

ALICE: 'E's asleep.

MAY: Wake up Rector.

The RECTOR *wakes up*.

RECTOR: Uh?

MAY: Sing it again, in English.

RECTOR (*sings*): Arise ye starvelings from your slumbers . . .

MAY: Stop! Stanly write it down. 'Arise ye starvelin's from your slumbers.'

STANLY: 'Oo got a pen?

ALL: I ab'm.

FARMERS: We, the farmers of this parish, have a cowlick.

One takes a cowlick from his pocket and hands it to GROSS.

MAY: Cowlick. Use that. 'Arise ye starvelin's from your slumbers.'

STANLY: 'Oo got paper?

MAY: On the wall! Write it on the wall!

GROSS *writes on the wall as the* RECTOR *sings the next line*.

RECTOR: Arise ye criminals of want . . .

MAY: Stop! 'Arise ye criminals of want.' Alice. Remember that . . . Go on rector.

RECTOR: For reason in revolt now thunders . . .

ALICE: 'Arise ye criminals of want.'

GROSS: 'Tis old language see.

MAY: Yaddap! 'For reason in revolt now thunders.' Stanly. Remember that.

RECTOR: And gone is the age of cant.

ALICE: Cant. Can't what?

RECTOR: Can't . . . go on . . .

He slumps back into unconsciousness.

MAY: Go on, that was the next two words.

GROSS: Dun't want they do 'e?

MAY: Thass the next line, start the next line. Go on, put 'em down, underneath. Go on.

GROSS: Go on.

MAY: Yes, go on, go on . . .

He writes it on the wall.

What we got thun?

They all stand back to look.

ALICE: Summin' about revolt.

MAY: 'Reason, in revolt, now thunders. Reason, in revolt, now thunders.' Thunder. Thunder. Thunder.

GROSS: That rhyme with slumber.

MAY: Slumber. Slumber. Slumber.

GROSS: 'Arise ye starlin's from your . . . lumber . . .' Thass it, tid'n slumber 'tis lumber. Tid'n starvelin's tis starlin's! Git up out the trees!

ALICE: What is starvelin' anyhow.

GROSS: Zactly, 'tis a warnin' . . . 'e'm tellin' we to bugger off . . . We'm the starlin's, arise, out the lumber, piss off 'ome 'e say, exit rapid through the winder!

ALICE: What winder?

GROSS: Damme through the door thun.

ALICE: Come on thun I dun't need tellin' twice.

MAY: Halt! Whas this 'criminals of want'. 'E'm tellin' we we done summin' wrong, we gotta sort out what that is. We can run now but they a catch up wi' we. We got unravel what we done!

STANLY: You knaw I got a feelin' I've 'eard this 'ere 'ymn before. Next verse got cockles in it.

MAY: Cockles!

STANLY (*sings*):
Go on, and bring home all the cockles,
Carry them humble to the font . . .

MAY: Awww Stanly . . .

STANLY: Charlie Bate used to play it on 'is accordion, down the ring o' bells . . .

MAY: Tis a bloody 'ymn!

ALICE: If we sing it, might make more sense . . .

MAY: Thass a damn good idea.

GROSS: Which version, starlin's?

MAY: Starvelin's. Stanly give us a key.

STANLY: Mmmmmmmmm.

ALL: Mmmmmmmmm.

MAY: Ready? And . . .

They start to sing the hymn. They sing it over and over. Sometimes there's a pause when they get to the end when they try to make sense of it, but always they start again. This can be heard in the far distance during the next scene. It's too distant to pick out the words, but the tune can be heard.

The Briefing Room. WALT, GILBERT, BUD, LIEUTENANT, *on another part of the stage.*

LIEUTENANT: Now. We're all fully briefed, and fed.

GILBERT: Yes thank you.

LIEUTENANT: Time Bud?

BUD: 22.30.

LIEUTENANT: Hm. Let's hear what they're saying to each other shall we? Before we go in?

He presses a button which activates a tannoy. The 'Internationale' can be heard through a tinny speaker. They strain to hear what's being sung.

My GOD! It's the *Internationale*! The arrogant bastards! The Communist anthem! On American soil! We got 'em!

GILBERT: Erm . . .

LIEUTENANT: What is it shithead!

GILBERT: Juss like to say that in our circles an International is a make of combine . . .

LIEUTENANT *jabs his finger at the tannoy*.

LIEUTENANT: That's what we're all here for! THAT'S WHAT WE'LL ALL DIE FIGHTING! HEAR ME?!

GILBERT: All right all right . . .

LIEUTENANT: Er, Gilbert, let me say something, at the end of all this we're gonna be heroes . . .

BUD: Singin's stopped.

LIEUTENANT: Uh? Oh. Yeah.

WALT: So what are we gonna do about 'em Lieutenant?

LIEUTENANT: We'll, ask 'em if they're Communists, if they say no, it's evident, with the information we've got, that they are lying. So we'll shoot 'em. Fall in.

They fall in.

Well men, this is the action we will all gain promotion for. I pray to God, that what we are about to do, is in the interest of democracy. Amen.

ALL: Amen.

LIEUTENANT: Let's do it.

They spring to attention, about turn, and are in the brig.

So, you even wrote it on the wall . . .

MAY: We 'ad to.

LIEUTENANT: Why?

MAY: Make out what it meant.

LIEUTENANT: The hell you didn't know . . .

MAY: Thass right we didn'.

STANLY: Still dun't.

LIEUTENANT: Tie their hands behind their backs.

MAY: Now just 'ang on 'ere . . .

LIEUTENANT: One move and we shoot. Now get up. Put your hands behind your backs. Tie 'em up Walt.

WALT *starts to tie them up*.

ALICE: Gilbert . . .

GILBERT: What?

ALICE: We still engaged?

GILBERT: We're about to break it off.

ALICE: They promoted you yet? To chief constable?

GILBERT: I'm retirin' next week. Earned enough now t'open up a restaurant.

ALICE: You was an agent thun.

LIEUTENANT: Cut the backchat willya?

ALICE: I just wanna know why we'm 'ere!

GILBERT: If mother . . .

LIEUTENANT: Wrap it Gilbert . . . You'll know soon enough.

WALT: Tied up sir.

LIEUTENANT: Now stand in line. One person moves, and Bud here has orders to shoot. He will shoot to maim. I don't want anyone dead until I've said what I have to say. OK Bud?

BUD: Er, yuh.

LIEUTENANT: Walt. What is the man doing with a gasmask on?

WALT: They were issued them in the last war, sir. There was a scare they might be gassed and they got to carrying them wherever they went. It became a kinda security symbol sir, if you wore your gasmask everything would be OK. Some never kicked the habit.

LIEUTENANT: After thirty-eight years?

WALT: I sucked my thumb till I was seventeen, sir.

LIEUTENANT: You sucked your thumb till you were seventeen?

WALT: I had it beaten outa me at boot camp sir, back in Okinawa, it's a strange psychological phenomenon, Freud touched on it, sir. It has to do with change and the shifting of the individual's status. We have to have a constant in our lives. Something we can refer to as we experience an ongoing, altering situation. It's practically unheard of in New Guinea, where civilisation hasn't altered or progressed for thousands of years.

GILBERT: I suck my tie when I'm 'ungry.

LIEUTENANT: Do you Gilbert? And how old are you?

GILBERT: Twenty-nine.

He takes the end of his tie and sucks it.

LIEUTENANT: Here, have a Nuttal's Mintoe.

He takes a Nuttal's Mintoe from his pocket and hands it to GILBERT, *who eats it.*

Now see here. Some days ago a body was washed up on these shores who we had reason to believe was a red infiltrator. We had been alerted to such invasions and our fears were confirmed when Gilbert her reported a Chinaman who passed himself off as a rector. We arrested this rector and sure enough confirmed his allegiance to Mao and duly brainwashed him back to sanity. On learning the fact that he had been preaching to the citizens of this parish in Chinese and you here apparently understood what he was saying we concluded that the insurgence had in fact been going on longer than we thought and this left us wondering just how far the damned thing had spread. In short we thought the best thing under the circumstances was to arrest everybody, in order to ascertain just who was or was not a pinko. Now I don't think, if evidence was ever needed, that we ever needed any more than what we have here. We have a tannoy system which is linked to the de-Brief Room and all of us here have witnessed over the last few minutes the most blatant evidence of allegiance to the Communist cause that I think I've ever had the misfortune to hear. However. I'm offering you all one last chance. I'm gonna ask you a simple question, and how you answer will, to a certain degree, determine your fate. The question is this. And I'll spell it out, nice and clear . . . Are, you, Communists?

ALL: NO!

LIEUTENANT: That's fine. Now Bud. Chamber a round, then shoot 'em. I think this will be messy, shall we walk out Walt, whilst Bud earns his stripe? In your own time Bud. See you for calisthenics . . .

He starts to walk out. BUD *chambers a round.*

WALT: Hold it Bud.

LIEUTENANT: Now what?

WALT: I'm relieving you of your command lieutenant.

The LIEUTENANT *stands down left, near the door, which is centre left.* WALT *is down right. The* PARISHIONERS *are ranged up centre with the* RECTOR *sitting in the middle,* BUD *is centre stage. He turns and faces downstage.* GILBERT *stands upstage of* WALT. *The* BODY *is near the* LIEUTENANT.

LIEUTENANT: On what grounds?

WALT: Certifiable evidence. United States Marines Small Units Tactics Manual Paragraph D62 subsection 10a paragraph one . . .

LIEUTENANT: I know the manual.

WALT: If an officer, due to excessive duty, shell-shock, battle fatigue or boredom displays a tendency beyond reasonable doubt towards psychopathy, schizophrenia or any allied mental disarray it is in the sympathy of supreme command for his under-rank to subsume seniority and take over command. Subject to military court proceedings at a later unnamed date.

LIEUTENANT: I KNOW THE FUCKING MANUAL!

WALT: Bud remove his insignia.

LIEUTENANT: Don't do it Bud.

WALT: Do it Bud!

BUD *does it.*

WALT: Now tie his hands behind his back and blindfold him.

BUD *does this. They speak as he does it.*

LIEUTENANT: You're making a mistake Bud.

WALT: I have proof Bud. Just do it then I'll prove it to you.

LIEUTENANT: He has no case Bud.

WALT: Tie him up Bud! Keep going!

The LIEUTENANT *is tied and blindfolded.*

Now gimme the weapon.

LIEUTENANT: Shoot him Bud.

WALT: Give it to me Bud.

BUD *walks towards* WALT, *hesitates*

centre stage as the LIEUTENANT *speaks.*

LIEUTENANT: He's wrong Bud I can have you court martialled and shot it's in the manual he has no case Bud shoot him Bud.

WALT: Don't listen to him.

LIEUTENANT: If there's any doubt in your mind Bud, any question at all, stick with me Bud . . .

WALT: Gilbert . . .

BUD *alerts*.

Easy Bud. Just gimme a chance. Gilbert.

GILBERT: Yuh?

WALT: You hide the body?

GILBERT: Er, yes.

WALT: Where?

GILBERT: 'Tis down Mother May's.

WALT: Go find Al. He's patrolling the weapons bunker. Have him run you down there in his Mitsubushi, pick up the body, bring it back here fast Gilbert run! Let him go Bud.

LIEUTENANT: Shoot him Bud!

WALT: This is evidence Bud.

GILBERT *goes*.

LIEUTENANT: What are you afraid of Bud? Sighta blood make you queasy? Never guessed you'd crack Bud. You're mustang material. Walt's cracked Bud but you Bud, you can hack it. You're a soldier, you're a man. A man, Bud, show us your skill, your training Bud, he's a pinko Bud, he's the enemy, we gonna let him get away with it Bud? Just you and me together Bud, there's no one left, think of the glory, the promotion, they don't promote you when you're dead Bud, you're a mustang. Please Bud please, this guy's a sergeant, d'you think he's told the half of it? Think he knows what I know? He ain't so smart Bud, he's a dime store philosopher Bud, he's got it all wrong, he's wrong and he knows it. I bin, I bin on the horn to Joint Chiefs Bud, they've bin expecting this, monitoring it Bud, we're all behind you Bud, the pogues, the heavies . . .

WALT: He's joshing you Bud, rear echelon know nothing of this!

LIEUTENANT: NO?

WALT: No! Wait for the body Bud!

LIEUTENANT: The whole of Europe's on a launch on warning did you know that Bud?

WALT: He's kiddin' ya!

LIEUTENANT: We gotta act fast, there's no time, shoot him Bud!

WALT: He's bullshittin' Bud he's delirious!

LIEUTENANT: Ignorant of this intelligence sergeant? You disappoint me.

WALT: OK, where we got to then, NSC?

LIEUTENANT: Beyond.

WALT: We got DCL?

LIEUTENANT: Negative. With SAC.

WALT: Joint Chiefs?

LIEUTENANT: On the horn to them.

WALT: Then call for a dust off!

LIEUTENANT: Too far down the pike sergeant.

WALT: You mean we got CPO's out there punched BYPASS!

LIEUTENANT: Tell me the time an I'll tell ya.

WALT: 22.55.

Silence.

Gimme bypass time if you have it.

LIEUTENANT: No dice.

WALT: You have it.

LIEUTENANT: No dice.

WALT: If you have it how do you know it? If we ain't got DCL! See Bud he's fucking kidding, now gimme the weapon!

LIEUTENANT: That's Nebraska. We have DCL with Kneecap.

WALT (*resigned*): OK, Lieutenant let's brute it out. The world is about to blow up Bud and he's second guessing me. Where will DCL take me?

LIEUTENANT: Joint Chiefs.

WALT: They on secure line?

LIEUTENANT: One way. After bypass time.

WALT: Then gimme bypass time.

Silence.

I gotta know bypass time for the right code.

Silence.

LIEUTENANT: Have yourself a sitdown sergeant. You're on rough turf. Is he sweatin' Bud? Weazel outa this one Walt. Boy, did he think he had it all wired down but he's weazling now, Bud, and I'm loving every minute. Every precious ticking minute.

WALT: You alerted Joint Chiefs?

LIEUTENANT: Uh-uh.

WALT: NSC?

LIEUTENANT: Nope?

WALT: JSTPS?

LIEUTENANT: Yup.

WALT: On the evidence of a dead body.

LIEUTENANT: And a tweed jacket.

WALT: You gotta be kidding lieutenant. You just gotta be kidding.

LIEUTENANT: There's no way a knowing Walt.

WALT: Bud.

BUD: Yuh?

WALT: You just let me put one call through to JSTPS. One call huh?

LIEUTENANT: Don't risk it, Bud.

BUD: I . . . I . . . dunnaw . . .

WALT: Bud. You're confused. You dunno who or what'n hell to believe. If I can prove to you Bud, just exactly ascertain who in hell you are, will you drop your weapon and allow me to make my call?

LIEUTENANT: What's your name Bud?

BUD: Bud.

LIEUTENANT: That's Bud.

WALT: Turn round Bud.

BUD *turns round. He's facing upstage, his back to the audience, facing the PARISH. They stare at him blankly. WALT moves up into BUD's eyeline, remains stage right. The BODY gives MRS MAY her cat.*

We don't have any time. Now I'm gonna ask you all a simple question. How you answer will, to a certain degree, determine your fate. The question is this. I'll spell it out, nice and simple. Do – you – know – this – man?

ALL: NO!

WALT (*disbelief*): Why do you say that? Why do you say it? Take your hat off Bud! Look at him! Look at him! (*Distraught.*) Drop your shoulders Bud! Look at him! Look at his face! Archie Gross for chrissake! He's your fucking son!

GROSS (*blankly*): I aren't Archie Gross. Archie Gross wouldn't lanc 'isself in the shit like 'iss. Archie Gross is a schemin', clever man. Archie Gross lead, where others follow. Archie Gross is a respected member of the community. Buster. I id'n no Archie Gross.

WALT: Mrs May! Look at him! Who is he!

MAY: Archie Gross. You kill my cat? He killed my cat. So it seem to me. While I was out' room. Wrung the bugger's neck. Dishin' up the tea.

WALT: Alice!

ALICE: Twad'n my fault 'e wore a tweed jacket. Too scared a what 'is mother might say. Too fond of 'is stomach.

WALT: Stanly!

STANLY *is asleep.*
(WALT *points at the* FARMERS.) YOU!

The following chorus occurs simultaneously with the ensuing dialogue, so WALT *speaks as soon as they start their rigmarole. They speak slowly and solemnly.*

FARMERS:
We, the farmers of this parish,
Smack our offspring
When they misbehave.
In the way our fathers taught us.
Hit back, they said,
And give as good as got.
We came to no harm.
And we acquiesced
In all our fathers said.
Our fathers were wise,
And their fathers' eyes
Though dead,

Were constantly upon them.
That way we keep
The generations steadfast.
We know what is right
Is right.
Because it happened
In the past.
We will never sway from that.

WALT: LOOK AT HIM! LOOK AT HIM! HE'S KENNETH! HE'S KENNETH! LOOK AT HIM!

LIEUTENANT: Its no use sergeant.

WALT: He's your own fucking flesh and blood! He was about to shoot you for . . .

He stops and realises what he's just said.

Sheeit.

AL *enters stage left. Behind the* LIEUTENANT, *opposite* WALT.

Al! Where's the body?

AL: What's goin on sarge?

WALT: WHERE'S THE BODY!

AL: Right out here, you wannit?

WALT: Bring it in here for fucksake you hear? Lay it out right there!

He indicates downstage centre. AL *goes out.* WALT *turns back to the* PARISH. *The* BODY *lies down where* WALT *indicated.*

Now. We have the body . . .

He sneaks a look downstage and sees the BODY. *He turns back and the* BODY *gets up and returns to where he came from. As* WALT *speaks,* AL *brings in* GRACE *and lays her out downstage. She is messy, covered in blood with one eye shot out.*

. . . I'm gonna ask Al to identify the body. He will tell us that it is Bud, whom we pitched over the cliff, and then I will ask Kenneth to tell us all who the fuck he is if that's Bud. Al tell us who the body is.

AL: I'm fucked if I know.

WALT *turns and sees* GRACE. BUD *turns too. The* FARMERS *stop speaking, silence.*

THAT'S THE WRONG FUCKING BODY! WHERE'S THE BODY!

BUD *is studying* GRACE, *recognition dawning.* AL *doesn't know what* WALT's *talking about.*

Where's Gilbert?

AL: That the cop?

WALT: For fucksake!

AL: He bought the ranch back there.

WALT (*incredulous*): You zapped him!?

BUD, *who has been studying* GRACE, *goes and kneels by her to take a closer look as they speak.*

AL: He's right out here you wannim brung in?

WALT: What you frag 'im for?

AL (*indicates* LIEUTENANT): He tole me to. Shoot on sight. Place was crawlin' with them.

WALT: Al . . .

AL: What's up with the looey? (*The* LIEUTENANT.)

WALT: He's cracked Al. Look we're busting heavies liberty call huh? Here's a dime, go play Space Invaders . . . gimme time to think, here's a dime, beat it!

He flicks AL *a dime and* AL *goes.* WALT *stands in the middle, confused. The* BODY *unties the* LIEUTENANT *but doesn't remove his blindfold. Music. As he unties the* LIEUTENANT, *he speaks to* WALT, *reminding him of an earlier deliberation.*

BODY:
The chemistry alters,
Warps the mind
And the minds of those
Around you.
Till it is I who is insane,
And the mad one, the psychopath,
Sane.

WALT *emerges from his reverie.*

WALT: Lieutenant. I was wrong. Down-rank me. Shoot all these people here. They are pinkoes. But please, we gotta call off bypass. Shoot 'em Bud, then we'll call off bypass. Is that a deal lieutenant?

LIEUTENANT: What's the time Walt?

WALT: 22.45.

LIEUTENANT: It could be a deal Walt, if we act fast.

BUD: 'Old on.

WALT: What?

BUD: This is Grace.

WALT: So what the fuck who it is Bud, c'mon, shoot 'em!

BUD: I'm not Bud. I'm Kenneth. This is Grace. My wife. Grace. What you shoot 'er for?

WALT: You heard Al, she was caught blowing up a United States weapons store, she's a pinko guerrilla Bud!

KENNETH: Look at 'er! Look at 'er!

He rises and walks to the LIEUTENANT, *who is still blindfolded. He screams in his face.*

LOOK AT HER!

The BODY *removes the* LIEUTENANT's *blindfold. The* LIEUTENANT *looks at his watch.*

LIEUTENANT: We have two minutes.

KENNETH: Don't move! Just tell me who I am. JUST TELL ME! Who I am! TELL ME! THAT'S MY WIFE! MY WIFE! TELL ME! WHO AM I! THAT'S GRACE! TELL ME! PLEASE TELL ME! WHO AM I?

WALT: You're Bud, Kenneth. Please, let me go.

WALT *makes for the door.*

KENNETH: DON'T MOVE!

LIEUTENANT: But, er, Kenneth, could we talk over this a little more amicably? In the comfort of the De-brief Room?

The LIEUTENANT *takes a tentative step forward.* KENNETH *is shaking. He raises his weapon.*

KENNETH: Don't come any closer. Is this my wife? Or is she a pinko guerrilla.

WALT (*quietly*): She's whatever you want her to be Bud. Need her to be. At any particular point in time.

KENNETH: What, what do I need her to be now? Tell me. Tell me. I need to be told.

The LIEUTENANT *looks at his watch.*

KENNETH (*screams*): DON'T MOVE!

LIEUTENANT: We have one minute Bud.

KENNETH: KENNETH!

WALT: Kenneth. She's no one you ever knew. She's no one. She doesn't matter anymore. To anybody. She is dead. Forget her and think of those around you who are alive.

The PARISH *has walked down stage and are standing close.* KENNETH *looks around at them.*

KENNETH: Who is she? Do you know her?

They all look at GRACE *and shake their heads.*

ALL: No.

KENNETH: Do you know me? Who am I?

They stare at him blankly. He stares back, at ARCHIE GROSS *naked and covered in mud,* STANLY *in his gasmask, the* RECTOR *dressed as a Chinaman,* MRS MAY *holding her dead cat,* ALICE *and the* FARMERS.

The lights dim to blackout as WALT *walks through the door.*

Bud, a US marine, died of boredom. Kenneth went missing picking mushrooms. Mrs May went cockling and found a dead body in the mud. Archie Gross went cockling and found a dead body in the mud. The same one. And Gilbert wore a tweed jacket to the dance. Grace went looking for Kenneth, her husband; he hadn't greased the combine. Mrs May claimed the body. She took it home. Archie Gross planned revenge. Up at the airbase Bud's uniform fitted Kenneth perfectly. (Walt, the sergeant, thought of everything). A Chinaman preached on the parish hall steps. The lieutenant smelled a rat. Archie Gross killed the cat. Grace's search for Kenneth took her to the fence. She was shot. Events drew close to the brink . . .

Nick Darke's first play, *Never Say Rabbit in a Boat* was performed at the Victoria Theatre, Stoke in 1978. Since then his plays have included *Landmarks* (Lyric Studio, Hammersmith), *A Tickle on the River's Back* (Theatre Royal Stratford East), *Say Your Prayers* (Riverside Studios, Hammersmith), *Summer Trade* and *The Lowestoft Man* (Orchard Theatre Company), and *The Catch* (Royal Court Theatre Upstairs). His one act play *High Water* was performed as a lunchtime production by the RSC in Newcastle and subsequently at The Warehouse. *Farmer's Arms,* a related play to *The Body,* is a *Play For Today. The Body* had its premiere on 22 April, 1983 at The Pit in the Barbican Centre. Nick Darke received the George Devine Award in 1979.

The RSC Playtexts are a joint publishing venture by the Royal Shakespeare Company and Methuen. This new series of programme texts is exclusively for productions at the RSC's small theatres: The Other Place in Stratford-upon-Avon; the Gulbenkian Studio for the Company's annual visit to Newcastle upon Tyne and The Pit in the Company's new London home in the Barbican Centre. The series aims to provide the theatregoer with a cheap, accessible and easily readable playtext and the author with a publishing opportunity where perhaps none before existed.

$ 5 95

ISBN 0 413 53340 9